The ABCs or Trail Riding and Horse Camping

–

Essential Knowledge for Trail and Camp

This is the book I wish I had when I started trail riding and camping with horses.

A TrailMeister Guide

The ABCs of Trail Riding and Horse Camping

ISBN: 978-1-7379315-0-8

Edited by Sue Haefliger and Valerie Lantz

A TrailMeister Guide
www.TrailMeister.com

Published by TrailMeister Press
PO Box 163, Newman Lake, WA 99025

Acknowledgments

Pride of authorship can't obscure that fact that no book is entirely the work of one person. Many people have provided invaluable assistance in the production of this manuscript, thank you to all who helped.

Celeste - My wife and my best friend. None of this would have been possible without you. Without you, there would be no acknowledgment page. Thank you.

Ed H. – You freely shared your skills and knowledge to help get me into the Wilderness and back again. I hope everyone has the good fortune to find friends and mentors like Ed who can help them "get out there".

Ken S. and Russ S. – You two are my "Bad Influences" who started the fire. I'm eternally grateful to both of you for introducing me to the joy of the high mountains and Wilderness. Without the two of you, I would not be here now, writing these words.

John H. – You've been the font of invaluable advice, an answerer of enumerable questions, and the one that drove ten hours to rescue me from a hospital in Montana after I broke myself.

Ruger, Ellie, Cocoa, LT, and Minning –You are better people than I am, even though you're mules and horses.

Neutral Language Statement
The term horse is used within to generically describe all equine beings, including mules and donkeys.

Table of Contents

A

ADVOCACY

A is for Advocacy, defined by our good friend Merriam-Webster as "the act or process of supporting a cause". Of course, the cause is keeping trails open to equestrian use.

Here are a few hard truths for you.

- Every day, a piece of paradise is paved and becomes a new housing development or shopping mall.
- State and Federal land managers have stagnant operating budgets and have a hard time keeping up with basic trail maintenance, let alone building new trail systems.
- Horse and mule riders are a very small population of trail users.

Unless you belong to a club, group, or organization that represents your interests as an equestrian, your voice isn't being heard. Many worthwhile groups will amplify your voice. Make an effort to find one that fits your needs. I am a member of the Back Country Horsemen organization, among others, but they are far from the only group working to ensure that trails remain open to stock use. Here are some options that will help make your voice heard.

Joining a local horse or mule club is a very effective way to help build and provide for the trails you love to ride. Your membership dues will often support not only your local groups' work but sometimes even nationwide efforts.

Most state horse councils (such as the Wisconsin Horse Council) provide a mouthpiece for equine owners to share ideas and suggestions on horse-related issues, organized trail rides, and other social functions. They also provide resources to promote the building and maintenance of bridle trails within the state.

The American Endurance Ride Conference (AERC) has a special Trails and Land Management Committee that provides grants for worthwhile trail building/maintenance projects on the trails that we ride.

The Equine Land Conservation Resource (ELCR) works through its members to raise awareness of the issues driving the loss of horse land and supports local actions to keep land open to equine use.

Already a member of an equine organization? Are they doing all they can to keep your trails accessible? Hold their hooves to the fire to ensure that your access to horse trails remains open.

ALPINE BUTTERFLY KNOT

The Alpine Butterfly, also known as the Lineman's loop, is a knot used to form a fixed loop in the middle of a rope. Tied in the

bight, the Alpine Butterfly can be made in a rope without access to either end. This is a distinct advantage when working with long ropes.

The butterfly is an excellent mid-line rigging knot; it handles multi-directional loading well and has a symmetrical shape that makes it

easy to inspect and untie. In a horse camping context, it is useful in highlines as an anchor point to tie on horses' leads.
See also Highlines, Knots

ANIMAL ENCOUNTERS

Hearing the high-pitched bugle of an elk, seeing the white specs of mountain goats above a rocky trail, and feeling the smooth muscles of a solid horse beneath you are a few of the many highlights of trail riding. Of course, some of the other animals that we sometimes hear about aren't quite so pleasant. Bears and other beasts have a mostly unwarranted reputation. Incidents do happen, but the fact of the matter is that you are much more likely to win the lottery than be the victim of a bear, cougar, or wolf attack. The critters I worry most about are ground wasps. These industrious creatures have caused more than one ride to turn into a rodeo and broken up many pack strings.
See also Bears, Insects, Pests

ANIMALS - FACTORS TO CONSIDER IN A TRAIL HORSE

Age and Experience - Age is always a factor in a trail horse. Younger is not necessarily better. With a seasoned animal, you can get on and go from day one. A healthy 10- or 12-year-old horse still has many good years left in him, and you'll enjoy the trails right away. If you want a better chance of avoiding problems on the trail, a horse with real experience is often worth a higher purchase price, especially if you are just starting on your outdoor riding adventures. An impromptu rodeo 10 miles from the trailer is no fun.

Of course, buying an older horse is no guarantee of a solid horse. There is no substitute for good disposition, training, and trail miles. For example, a 4-year-old horse with lots of trail miles under him might be a better choice than a 15-year-old who rarely leaves the barn lot. The younger animal has a solid foundation to continue building upon, where the inexperienced beast will have a steep learning curve.

Gender – Any time choices for trail horses are discussed, the topic of mare or gelding comes up. The conversation can get heated quickly. Both can be excellent mounts, and although I ride a gelding, I try hard not to get too stuck on one or the other and instead place a  heavy emphasis on the animal's personality. Many people say that geldings are the only way to go, but I've had the pleasure of being in the company of some outstanding mares. For me, it's not an issue. I've seen mares that seem to bond with their riders better than a gelding might. Again, I think it comes down to an individual's personality. I would avoid a stallion as a trail mount. He might be very well behaved, and the most excellent beast at the stable, but all of those good qualities can fly out the window in an instant on the trail.

Personality or Disposition - The most important trait that I'm looking for is a good disposition. A horse with a kind and willing disposition is much easier to work with and train for the myriad of challenges that it will be asked to face. Unless you like drama on your rides, look for a horse that is neither over-reactive nor has an overly high flight instinct. A calm yet willing disposition will help a good trail horse stand quietly while tied, remain calm on the edge of a mountain, and get along with other horses in camp (as well as cows, dogs, elk, and deer).

Conformation and Health – This is an area where I look to the experts. The animal you're considering may seem perfect. But to make an informed decision and help decide if you can live with its inevitable flaws, an unbiased clinical evaluation from a medical professional is crucial. Make sure that your veterinarian has a clear understanding of what jobs the prospect will be expected to perform. No animal is perfect, and if examined rigorously enough, faults will be found. Knowing what the animal's job will be will help the doctor determine if she'll be sound and serviceable for those tasks. Pre-purchase exams aren't pass / fail tests. They are simply a data set that helps you as a buyer to make the most informed decision.

Finding Cocoa

I've said for years, to many thousands of people worldwide, that I thought the perfect trail mount would be an Icelandic Mule. I found one while leading trail riding clinics in Canada. Meet Cocoa.

Cocoa is a 13.1 hand molly mule out of an Icelandic mare. She was 14 years old and as green as grass when I met her. The entirety of her job to date had been to be cute and eat apples. Cocoa was VERY good at being cute and eating apples.

There's a lot more to helping a mule find the great trail mount within than being cute and eating apples. They need to pass many disposition and health checks before they come home.

Before meeting Cocoa, furry face to furry face, I had many questions for her owner. I think every potential buyer needs to ask these initial questions, at a minimum, of every seller of an animal.

What's her disposition like?
I'm not a fan of drama, so words like "kind, curious, sweet, and easy-going" are essential to me.

What does she do or has been asked to do?
Had I not been looking for an opportunity to train, I would have passed on an animal whose only job has consisted of "being cute and eating apples". For most trail riders, I would ask about what experiences and training the animal has had.

How does she interact with other members of the herd?

Cocoa's position at the bottom of the herd pecking order was a good thing as I believe that such animals are habituated to following a leader. They're content to stay in the background and avoid any heated encounters. I will need to be a good and benign leader for her.

How does she interact with people?

Hearing "pocket pony" made a lot of sense especially given her job of being cute. However, having an 800lb animal in your space begging for apples may not be a good thing. I like critters to respect my personal space unless I ask them to approach, not before.

What's her medical history look like?

Ask about vaccination history, deworming information, recent Coggins testing, dental exams, last teeth floating, and any medical issues. The owner was very forthcoming about a stifle issue, and that other than Cocoa was due for a pedicure and vaccinations, she reported no problems.

Once these initial questions were satisfactorily answered it was time for an in-person interview.

APPS – MAPPING / TRACKING

There are myriads of applications for your cell phone that purport to tell you where you are and where to go. Until the phone breaks, runs out of battery power, or loses its signal. Feel free to use these technological wonders but take the time and the effort to understand the basics of how they do what they do before you blindly trust your life to them. At a minimum be able to use a traditional map and compass.

See also GPS, Maps, Navigation

AWARENESS

How many people are riders, and how many are passengers? Just as our mounts need to be aware of their surroundings, so must we. A rider is aware of everything that is going on. A passenger is just cargo for the horse to pack. Be attentive to your mount and what he's thinking. A healthy awareness of your animal and your surroundings will help keep you safe and secure.

See also Terrain Association

B

BALING TWINE
Baling twine is the duct tape of the horse-owning world. It fixes just about everything.

Here are six reasons to keep baling twine in your saddlebags.

Belt - When your pants get loose, a baling twine belt is sometimes the only thing between you and droopy drawers. Whether you braid your belt from 12 strands or stick with a single piece, a baling twine belt could save the day.

Emergency halter - Halters break, usually right when you need them most. Baling twine halters work and are easy to make.

Lead rope - Make your lead ropes using braided baling twine or fasten a quick release knot to make an emergency lead or tie for your animals.

Shoelaces - When a shoelace gives out, there is only one acceptable solution - baling twine.

Measuring device - Not everybody carries a measuring tape with them at all times. A piece of twine is an excellent way to gauge sizes in the field or take measurements of an animal for later comparison.

Tack repair - On the trail, riders have to make do with what they have. Those who travel with baling twine know that they're ready in the event of tack malfunctions. Baling twine can repair anything from broken reins and bridles to stirrup leathers.

BEAR BELLS
Bear bells are small bells that serve to alert bears, and other animals, of your presence so that you don't accidentally startle them.

It's the surprise meetings between bears and riders that can lead to a tense standoff or, potentially, an attack. As your horse moves, the bell will inevitably jingle loud enough that anyone or anything in the immediate area can hear it.

Other bear prevention methods: Talking/Singing: One of the cheapest and easiest bear deterrents is talking or singing while you ride. Bears associate voices with humans, and they will often take cover when they hear you coming. My go-to song is "itsy bitsy spider". When I sing this, I'm guaranteed to repel both bears and humans!

BEAR CANISTERS
A bear rummaging through camp could cut your trip short and endanger both you and the bear. You can avoid those situations by storing attractants properly in a bear canister.

Also known as bear cans or bear vaults, these devices are bear-resistant containers whose primary purpose is to protect your food from bears, rodents, and other wild animals. They may be hard or soft and come in a wide variety of shapes and construction types.

Store bear canisters at least 100 yards from your camp. Make sure that the canister is secure and fully closed. Keeping the canister locked and closed will help reduce food odors in the area and prevent attracting nearby bears. NOTE: Most bear canisters don't keep all odors locked in but rather make it too difficult for a bear to get to the items of interest and realize any food rewards.

If you're camping anywhere there may be the potential for bear activity or any other wild animals, a bear canister is a good idea. Beyond that, bear canisters are required in many regions. Know the rules for the area that you're going to be camping in.

The phrase "better safe than sorry" is a cliche for a reason. I  recommend using a bear canister to avoid interactions with "mini-bears" such as raccoons and chipmunks. Even if there are no regulations where you plan to camp, it will help reduce the risk of attracting ursine or other visitors looking for an easy meal.

While you may think food is the only thing you'll be keeping in a bear canister, there are a few other items you'll want to store in there as well. Anything with a smell that could spark a bear's interest should be kept in the container; this includes food, toothpaste, toiletries, lip balm, and sunscreen.

BEAR SAFETY TIPS
Although bear attacks are very uncommon and black bears rarely become aggressive when encountered, it's best to avoid bears by

following these simple steps.

1) Store bear canisters at least 100 yards from your tent.
2) Cook, eat, and clean at least 100 yards from your tent.
3) Brush your teeth away from camp and keep scented hygiene products in the canister with your food.
4) Be bear aware. Be alert, make noise, and stay on trails.
5) Bring bear spray and know how to use it.
6) Finally, Leave No Trace!

Most bears stay away from people. Most campers never know that they've been near a bear because bears do a great job of avoiding us. If you should see a bear, don't panic. Most encounters end with the bear and human departing in opposite directions, without harm to either. The chance of being hurt by a bear is lower than your risk of being hit by lightning. The risk is also lower than the chance of a car accident on your way to the trailhead.

BEAR SPRAY

While many gun proponents remain adamant that firearms offer better protection against a charging bear than pepper spray, scientific research suggests otherwise.

> PRO TIP
> ### Do not pre-spray objects with bear spray.
> If used this way, it may actually attract a bear because of the residue's strong odor.

Bear spray is a non-lethal deterrent designed to stop aggressive behavior in bears. Its use can reduce human injuries caused by bears and the number of bears killed by people in self-defense. Bear spray uses a fine cloud of red pepper oil (oleoresin of capsaicin) derivatives to temporarily reduce a bear's ability to breath, see, and smell, giving you time to leave the area.

BLANKETING YOUR HORSE

I'm constantly chilled during the winter months as I feed, care for, and ride my animals, and I frequently wonder if I should pull out the blankets. I'm not the only one wondering about blanketing. Rather than give you hard and fast "rules" about when and when not to put a blanket on, I've developed some guidelines to help you determine what's best for your horse.

Before we consider the blanket let's think about the animal. Equines of all types are masters at staying quite comfy in weather that sends us running for our coats. You cannot determine a horse's need for a blanket by how chilly you feel. It just doesn't work like that.

The primary method that keeps a horse warm is eating. Our horses' favorite activity is helping keep them warm. Heat is a byproduct of the digestion process, so on a frigid night, the first thing we should think of is providing our beasts with plenty of hay to keep that equine furnace burning. Centered in the horse's  hindgut is an internal furnace where microbes convert the fiber in the hay into energy with heat created as a byproduct. It's a pretty darn nifty process if you ask me. Of course, the digestion process also needs water to keep running, so make sure to keep the H2O ice-free and, even better, not ice cold.

A secondary characteristic that helps keep the cold at bay is the size of the animal. While you could steal your kid's science book for a physics primer on why this is, it's easier to think of a large block of ice that takes longer to thaw than a smaller chunk; a large body stays warmer longer than a small one.

We share the third winter warmth feature with our trail partners, although they're much more efficient than we are. Horses and mules use the same process that we call Goose Bumps to stay warm. The tiny muscles attached to each hair follicle contract and cause the hair strands to literally "stand on end". This creates a surprisingly warm layer of air around the animal. If you don't believe that, you've never held your hand under a mane on a cold day. The reason behind this is another physics lesson on the second law of thermodynamics. This layer of warm air is essentially the same as the loft in a sleeping bag. Did you know that a blanket could make your horse colder by squashing this natural insulating layer of hair? If you compress that loft with a heavy blanket that removes the air voids, he can get cold quickly. Keep that in mind in borderline situations where he may be more comfortable wearing his natural blanket than a store-bought one.

So even though it may be frigid out, if your horse is in good condition, eating plenty of roughage, and wearing his own hair coat, he's probably going to be toasty warm as long as he can stay dry and isn't in direct wind.

Now that we've discussed a perfect world, let's talk about the less than optimum world that we live in.

Here's a quote from the docs at the Veterinary Medicine and Biomedical Sciences Department at Texas A&M University. "For the vast majority of horses, it will never be too cold for them to live outside with no blanket", "Horses survive in very harsh winter environments with their natural hair coat. Those horses that would benefit from blanketing are those that are thin, debilitated, ill, or have no natural hair coat".

Not every horse has a warm wooly coat. Some breeds have naturally thin coats, and others have thin coats from blanketing, living in a warm climate or barn, or have a coat that has been clipped. The further you get from optimum, the more you should consider adding a blanket. You'll also have to consider if the animal is underweight, isn't eating enough roughage, isn't able to get out of the wind or rain or has a health concern that compromises his ability to stay warm.

On the furthest reaches of optimum is the case of show animals that are kept artificially thin coated to be ready for presentation. These animals should certainly have a blanket to help them stay warm in winter.

Closer to home for trail riders is the case of wind and rain. The weather is rarely optimal; when it is, wait a few minutes, and it'll change. Wet animals lose body heat very quickly as the wind increases and temperatures drop. Snow is not as hard on our friends as an icy rain because a layer of snow on the horse's back acts as an insulator. For our animals in this environment, we try to avoid blankets when we're able and instead opt for shelters that they could use to escape the rain and wind.

When I'm considering blanketing, these are the guidelines I consider before I pull the blankets out.

- Is the animal visibly uncomfortable or shivering?
- Is he older, weak, ill, or recovering from an illness?
- Is he very young?
- Is he clipped?
- Is he going to be shown?
- Is he lacking a sufficient winter coat?
- Did he recently move from a warmer climate to a cooler climate?

If the answer is yes to any of these, I'll put a blanket on. If not, I don't bother, and the horse is more content and much happier as a result.

BOOTS – HOOFWEAR

Hoof boots provide an alternative to traditional horseshoes. Some of

the benefits are that boots are removable, offer complete hoof coverage, are flexible, and allow traction to vary as conditions change. Modern hoof boots are made of strong and flexible materials that support and protect a barefoot animal. I use hoof boots mainly in the shoulder seasons when day rides are the norm, and I have plenty of time to put them on my animals.

Proper fit is paramount for success with hoof boots. Boot manufacturers are very willing to help determine the correct size for your horse. Take measurements and tracings of your horse's feet immediately after trimming. By tracing your horse's foot, you'll clearly see the shape. Keep in mind that hoofs vary in shape, especially from front to back.

BOOTS – HUMAN FOOTWEAR
Proper footwear when riding and camping with horses is important. Suitable footwear for horse riders and those camping with horses includes heavy construction to protect your feet if a horse steps on you, as well as a prominent heel to keep your foot from sliding through a stirrup. Trail riders and campers also need to consider how comfortable their boots are when on the ground. I look for boots with enough tread to keep me from slipping while walking but not so much traction that my foot gets caught in the stirrup.

BOWLINE – THE KING OF KNOTS
The bowline is one of the oldest knots on record, and for a good reason. It's easy to tie and untie even when under load. When I'm horse camping, I use the bowline as a vital anchor point for highlines.

When tying the bowline, an easy way to remember the process is to imagine the end of the rope as a rabbit and repeat the rhyme: "Up through the rabbit hole, round the big tree; down through the rabbit hole and off goes he". *See also Highline, Knots, Online Resources*

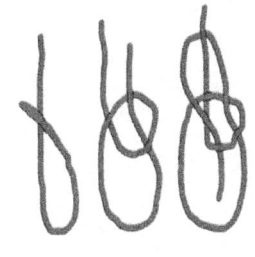

BREAST COLLAR

The breast collar, or breastplate, is a piece of tack used to keep the saddle from sliding back when moving uphill. The breast collar also serves an essential safety purpose; to stop the saddle from rolling under the belly if a cinch breaks. For riding in hilly areas, I think a breast collar and britchen are must-have pieces of tack.

See also Britchen, Crupper

BRIDLE

The second most fundamental part of your horse's tack. Used to help provide direction, the bridle aids in control and communication with your animal. Leather is the most common material but requires significant maintenance. Synthetics are easy to care for and last seemingly forever.

BRITCHEN

Britchen, or breeching, is a broad strap that goes around an animal's haunches to keep saddles from sliding forward when going downhill. The function of britchen is similar to that of a crupper, but I believe it is much kinder to my animals.

A wide strap across a horse's hip has more area to help distribute rider

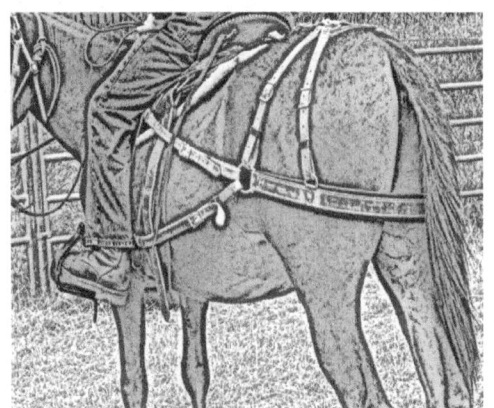

and saddle weight than a crupper's thin band under the tail. Dispersing the pressure helps your horse be more comfortable while also keeping your saddle from slipping forward.

With a britchen's multiple straps,

a custom-fit is easy to obtain for any horse. I've added britchen to all of my saddles, both riding and pack, and I believe my animals are happier for the change.

See also Crupper

BUGS

Any of a variety of creepy crawlies that conspire to make us, our horses, miserable during trail rides and camping trips.

See also Insects, Pests

BUMPER PULL - TRAILER

These are the most common type of horse trailers. The name is a bit misleading as the hitch isn't connected to the vehicle's bumper but rather to the much more substantial frame.

Bumper pull trailers offer many advantages. Most bumper pulls are smaller than goosenecks. This means a bumper pull trailer usually costs less than a gooseneck. The small size also means you may be able to use a smaller truck for towing. First-time trailer owners will also appreciate that a bumper pull trailer has a normal turn radius, so the trailer will follow the towing vehicle as it takes a turn.

Bumper pull trailers do have disadvantages. A smaller trailer means less space and limits the number of animals and the amount of gear you can transport. As with most horse owners, my first trailers were bumper pulls. As I started going on longer trips and hauling more animals, I moved to a gooseneck style, which gave me an excellent excuse to buy a bigger truck.

See also Gooseneck, Trailer

C

CAMPING – WHY HORSE CAMP

We love our horses and mules. We love trail riding, and we love being outdoors. What could be better? Camping. While there is certainly something to be said for crashing on the couch and binge-watching British costume dramas, visiting a horse camp and living outdoors for a few days with our animals just an arm's length away is much more appealing. Horse camping is a way to be adventurous, make memories of a lifetime, and spend quality time with impressive people. Here are six more reasons to try it!

It's Healthy - Camping does a body good. Nearly every aspect of camping provides health benefits, from being more active, getting more natural light, fresh air, improved mental health, and more. Research shows that time spent outdoors can improve your blood pressure, improve digestion, and even give your immune system an extra boost. When you spend a few days outside, you'll get some serious health benefits.

It's Tradition - Horse camping is an activity steeped in history and tradition. Images of cowboys warming themselves by the campfire after a long day on the trail create powerful urges within us to go out and recreate those scenes. When we're in a horse camp, I like to think of the people who decades ago decided that this spot would be perfect for camping with stock and then built it.

It's Immersion in Nature - Any equine camping, whether it's a tent deep in the backcountry or parking the LQ at a guest ranch, is an enveloping experience. You'll see wildlife in their natural settings, and you'll enjoy million-dollar views from your tent or trailer door. You'll feel the sun on your face (as well as the rain and the wind!). The stars: oh, the celestial bodies that you'll view on a dark night. The sounds: the soft crunch of the ponies contentedly chewing hay to the yips of the coyotes in the distance and the trills of songbirds flitting through camp. You'll experience many marvelous feelings in nature!

It'll Put You in a Good Mood - Researchers have linked  outdoor activities to a decrease in depressive thoughts. The feeling of happiness that you get when you take your first breath of air at the campground is because of the burst of serotonin that you get from the extra oxygen of the outdoors. Sleeping under the stars also helps you get in touch with your natural circadian rhythms, a foundation for high-quality sleep and health.

It's a Digital Detox - Sometimes, you need a break from technology. It might be hard to escape it at home, but most parks and campgrounds have poor or no cell connections. Horse camps are perfect places to put down the high-tech devices in our lives and focus on the basics. Sit back and relax with a good book, write in a journal, or enjoy watching the horses graze. Use this digital downtime as a way to connect with nature and reconnect with each other. Time without electronic distractions forces you to connect with others and with yourself, which is a pretty fantastic experience.

It's New Challenges and Life Skills - No two camping trips are the same, and that's good. A University of Michigan study shows that new experiences help keep our brains healthy. New physically and intellectually stimulating activities have the most significant effect on brain health, and horse camping fits both of these criteria. Camping also makes you rely on yourself to meet your basic needs, purifying water, making a fire, etc. Building these skills gives you confidence and self-worth that carries over into all other aspects of your life. It just takes a little effort and guidance, and you'll be setting up tents in no time!

CARABINERS

These tools are a mainstay in mountain climbing and emergency rescue communities. Carabiners have a permanent home in my trail and camping kits.

Generally speaking, a carabiner is a coupling link with a safety closure, meaning it's basically a tool designed to hold two things together. It does this through a curved body with a straight or curved bar, known as the gate, that opens and closes.

A locking carabiner has a gate reinforced with a locking mechanism; this secures the carabiner in its closed position and ensures absolute safety. I use locking carabiners anytime there's a chance that a horse could get either itself or its tack caught. The small extra cost is well worth the peace of mind.

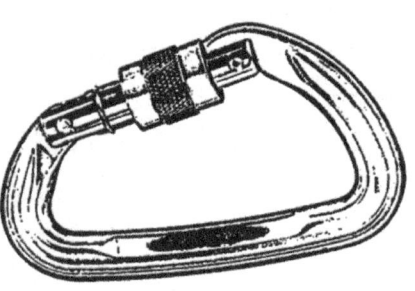

It's worth noting that not all carabiners are the same. Those found in the checkout lane of the feed store are rarely robust enough for use around horses and mules. The presence of a climbing rating on your carabiners means that they are strong enough to withstand at least 20 kilonewtons (kN) or 4,496 pounds. The safety of my animals, and me, is essential. I only use carabiners rated for climbing.

PRO TIP

Carabiners approved for climbing will be certified with a CE or UIAA icon

Cheap carabiners found in the checkout aisle may not hold your keys without failing.

CHAPS

Chaps aren't just for cowboys. These sturdy leg coverings offer protection from brush and weather. Heavy leather chaps provide excellent abrasion resistance but tend to become waterlogged even when oiled. Lightweight synthetics are excellent at repelling water but can be quickly shredded by trailside brush. I've been pleased with sturdy oilskin chaps that both repel water from morning dew or sudden downpours and protect my legs from scrub along the trailside.

CINCH

The idea behind this vital piece of tack is misleadingly simple: Hold the saddle in place so that it's comfortable and safe for horse and rider. Anyone who has ever had a cinch or girth fail and found themself suddenly sideways, upside down, or on the ground will tell you that it is essential to select the right cinch. A horse who has had to endure chafing, pinching, or the painful constriction of a poorly designed or ill-fitting cinch or girth would agree. A good cinch can make the difference between a great ride and a long walk home.

A primary concern in selecting a cinch or girth is its material. Various materials offer significant benefits such as softness, sweat absorption, resistance to slipping, and easy maintenance. Some materials have downsides that need to be considered, such as lack of durability, a tendency to cause galls, an affinity for brush and burrs, or too little give. You'll want to know what a cinch is made from, as well as the characteristics of the material.

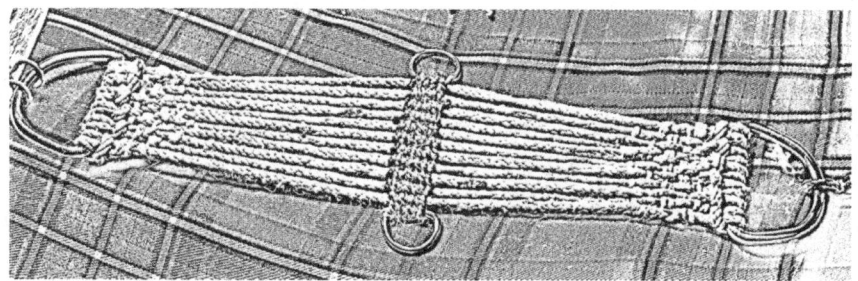

A few popular materials found in cinches are:
- Polyester is cheap and doesn't hold seeds and burrs but neither does it breathe, or wick sweat.
- Neoprene is very easy to clean and doesn't attract burrs. However, neoprene doesn't give, is easily over tightened, and doesn't breathe.

- Wool and wool blend string girths all breathe, and wick sweat well. They resist collecting burrs and seeds and rarely cause soring when used properly.
- Fleece attracts grass seeds and burrs like a magnet. If you use a fleece girth you should quickly get in the habit of checking to ensure that nothing that could gall your horse is caught in the fleece.
- Those that ride Australian or English saddles have the option of leather girths. Leather is easy to clean, gives slightly, and doesn't hold burrs and trail detritus.

Fortunately, cinches are relatively inexpensive. If your current cinch isn't working, it's easy to try a different one.

Although it may be counterintuitive, I've had good experiences with narrow string cinches that fit better in the horse's cinch "pocket" and don't create any sore-producing wrinkles.

CINCH - FLANK
A double-rigged saddle without a functional back cinch is like a suitcase with only one latch buckled.

The rear, or flank, cinch is more than a pretty accessory for a Western saddle. It's a safety feature that holds your saddle snug to your horse's barrel and prevents the cantle from tipping forward.

For trail riding in areas where

there are hills, the back cinch is a must. You also need to set it up properly. I see many riders with back cinches hanging far below their horses' bellies, which makes me cringe. Anything from a hoof to a stick could go through that empty space and be the cause of an "eventful" ride. I prefer to avoid "eventful" rides.

I like my rear cinch tighter than just touching. It's not as tight as the front cinch but slightly more than snug. A cinch's job is to secure the saddle; if it's loose, it'll have that much further to travel before it engages. I tend to put the back cinch behind the largest part of the belly for my mules to help keep the saddle from sliding forward. No, this isn't a bucking strap. A cinch hobble connecting the front cinch to the rear keeps the cinch from migrating too far back. Indeed, if you're using a flank cinch, you'd better have that hobble attached lest you become the cause of a "sporty" event.

CLOTHING

Dusty trails and horse camps may not be fashion show settings, but what you wear does matter. Your choice of attire directly impacts your safety and comfort. Be prepared for weather changes; wearing a cotton shirt on a sunny 70-degree day is great, but when you're caught in a rain shower, that cotton shirt will chill you to the bone.

Headgear – I'm a firm believer in helmets when riding. That being said, it's a free country, and you're free to do what you will. Traditional cowboy hats offer a break from the sun that is very welcome on hot days.

See also Helmet

Shirts – Avoid overly loose garments that can catch and hang up on tack or tree branches. Even in the heat of Summer, I wear long sleeves to protect against the sun and insects.

Pants – Jeans are ubiquitous on the trail and in camp. You want to avoid pants that twist, wrinkle, or bunch along the inside of your legs and especially knees. Again, your trousers should not be too large as they may catch on something, leading to injury to yourself or your horse.
See also Chaps

COMMUNICATIONS
Communicating with the folks back home while you're camping seems like the last thing you would want to do. After all, we've left technology behind to embrace the wilderness. There's no better feeling than being "off the grid", disconnected from the outside world.

However, there are exceptions to this; you may have health problems, family members that need checking on, or you may need up-to-date information for the trip home. In these circumstances, having access to reliable communications while camping in remote locations is not only a good idea but a necessity.

When you're out in the wild and need to call for help, don't be surprised if your cellphone reads "No Service". Backcountry communicators are, at their best, lifesaving devices that allow you to check in with friends and family back home and reach emergency services in a pinch, even when you're far off the grid.
See also Emergency Plan, Personal Locator Beacons, Satellite Messengers

Be sure to educate all involved before your trip on what to expect when tracking your progress with satellite messengers.

If they don't know how these devices operate, they may alert rescue teams when they are not needed.

When Good Communications Saved the Day

While in the Pasayten Wilderness, along the Canadian border, where cell coverage is just a dream, we noticed a thick smoke plume, and haze started filling the basin where we had set up camp. The plume was to the southeast. It was also the

direction of our only route back to civilization. If the road were closed, our weeklong trip might turn into something much longer. We needed wildfire info ASAP to make an informed decision on the safest option.

I sent a satellite message to our emergency contact at home to see if he could find any wildfire info. Within minutes we had a situation report on the fire and where it was heading (across the only road into the trailhead). With that information, we were able to make a plan. We would break camp at first light, ride 12 miles to the trailhead, and immediately depart for home. I shared our data with some hikers camped nearby so that they could make informed decisions for themselves.

By the time we made it to the trailhead the next afternoon, the smoke was getting thicker. A quick set of messages on the SatPaq let us know that the road out was clear at the moment, but the wind forecast had the fire line heading across it. We needed to leave ASAP. And we did!

When we reached the bottom of the mountain and back onto paved roads, the impact of the fire was clear; Mountainsides that were green a few days before were blackened and still smoking. The fire line was a half-mile away from a critical intersection where we had to go. The surrounding area was crisscrossed with red streaks from aerial fire-retardant drops.

We were never in immediate danger. But had the wind shifted, it could have become interesting in short order. With the SatPaq, we had access to the data that allowed us to make informed decisions.

COMPASS

Modern GPS technology is beneficial. However, it's far from foolproof. Consider this. What if your GPS breaks? How will you find your way back to the trailhead? A magnet on a stick will give you important clues.

A compass is a simple tool that remains important even in this era of high technology. Every trail rider and backcountry camper should know how to use this still vital device.

Types of Compasses:

While several types of compasses are available, two models stand out as standard equipment for riders and other outdoors enthusiasts: the lensatic compass and the orienteering, or baseplate compass.

While the lensatic model is a standard issue for the U.S. military, it is heavy and requires more practice to become proficient. The information that follows is based on the baseplate or orienteering style since it is both the least expensive, most common and the more easily used of the two. However, the basic concepts involved in navigation apply to both types.

At first glance, a compass may seem a bit daunting. Covered in various markings and with multiple moving parts, it seems to demand a high level of skill to operate. Quite to the contrary, with a little bit of knowledge of the primary functions, anyone can work an orienteering compass like a pro.

At its heart, every compass consists of a magnetized metal needle that floats on a pivot point, and the needle orients to the earth's magnetic field.

PRO TIP

A compass is essentially a magnet on a stick.

Its readings can be affected by the presence of ferrous (iron and steel) objects.

The Basic Orienteering Compass is Composed of the Following Parts:

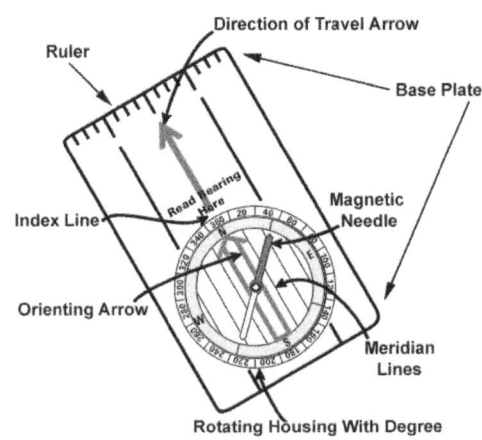

- Base plate – Clear is good to read the map
- Straight edge and ruler
- Direction of travel arrow
- Compass housing with 360-degree markings
- North label
- Index line – Located above the bezel, it's also called a "read bearing here" mark
- Orienting arrow – Used to orient the bezel, it has an outline shaped to exactly fit the magnetized end of the needle. – Remember the rhyme "Red in the Shed", I like to think of it as a "horse in the barn"

- Orienting lines – Parallel lines that rotate with the bezel; aligning these with the north-south lines on a map aligns your orienting arrow with the map's North
- Magnetic needle – North end is red

CONFIDENCE

We trail ride and camp with our horses because there is nothing better in the world than enjoying the outdoors with our furry friends. Yet, it's not always perfect.

When you're in any situation (riding or otherwise), the more prepared you are, the more confident you'll feel. This preparedness and confidence will help you stay out of trouble. Confidence also helps you feel more capable of controlling yourself and your horse in stressful situations.

Following are the tools that I use to improve my confidence. They'll work for you as well.

CONFIDENCE IN THE SADDLE

Many riders with confidence issues tend to focus on the problems they're having when they're in the saddle when in reality, the problems began on the ground.

Take, for example, a horse that doesn't stand quietly when you get in the saddle. It can be intimidating as well as an inconvenience and a safety issue. Issues like this have one common denominator. The animal doesn't respect you.

The process of earning your horse's respect starts on the ground as you teach your horse to respond to your cues. As your horse learns to respect your rules through groundwork, you'll see those same lessons carry over to your riding. A friend of mine, Mule Clinician Ty Evans, elucidated this concept with this question. "If your mule doesn't listen to you when you're on the ground, why on earth would it listen when you're on its back?" This concept also applies to horses!

Groundwork is about establishing better control over your horse's movements. As your animal learns to recognize your cues and respond accordingly, the horse will better understand your expectations and be used to following your lead. As you teach your horse to respect your rules through groundwork, you'll see those lessons will carry over when you're in the saddle. You'll also grow more confident in the saddle with a clear understanding of how your horse moves and responds.

In your relationship with your horse, there needs to be a leader, and that leader needs to be you. You're the only one in the partnership who knows the plan. After all, you're the one who knows whether you're turning right or left at the next trail junction, where to cross the river safely, or where your camp is for the night.

The key to communicating with your horse and making yourself the leader—is consistency and repetition. Start at the beginning and take it slowly. Pay as much attention to the small details of horsemanship as you do to your animal's health. If Cocoa wants to take a step when I'm loading the pack saddle, thank you for the opportunity! We'll practice moving our feet until she's re-learned that when the saddles are out, it's work time. We practice this at home so that it's not an issue at the trailhead.

See also Groundwork

CONFIDENCE WHEN CAMPING

Practice, practice, practice. You might have a ride in mind that involves camping midway through, or there could be an urge to spend some quality time at an established horse camp.

PRO TIP

My first camping trip of every year is in the back pasture.

It's best to test new pieces of gear and ensure the critters are ready for camping, close to home rather than several hours away.

Camping adventures give you incredible diversity in options for your trips, allowing you to access areas that may not be possible when your house is your base camp. It's also easy to make mistakes that could derail your enjoyment. That's why it's essential to feel confident in what you're doing so you can concentrate on the reasons why you decided to do this in the first place. The sense of achievement from being in the wide open and possibly having pushed yourself out of your comfort zone is incredible!

Just as we become more confident with every additional minute spent in the saddle, we become more optimistic in camp through more camping experiences.

When I set up camp in the back pasture, I pretend that I'm 20 miles inside the Bob Marshall Wilderness Complex, not 800 feet from a hot shower. Set up camp the same way you would in a "real" situation, and you'll soon learn what works and what doesn't.

Slow is smooth, smooth becomes fast. Don't rush to failure.

Take your time when you're addressing a new skill set, such as leading a pack mule, tying a double diamond, or any other part of trail riding and camping. Be slow and deliberate. When we rush into situations that we're not ready for, we forget to check the fine points, and we all know that it's the details that count. Start at the beginning and gradually work your way through.

If you've never horse camped before, don't start planning a 2-week pack-trip right away. Work up to those bucket list adventures in small steps. Practice makes proficient, and proficiency leads to perfection. Take your time, really practice, and work towards your goal, whatever it is.

Before you move forward, your current skills should be smooth and relaxed for you and your horse. Be deliberate, don't rush to failure, acknowledge the progress you've made, clap for yourself, and keep pushing forward! Once you've done the basics, then you're probably ready. If you're confident, your horse will be as well.

Mistakes are proof that you are trying.

Despite what some on social media may declare; everyone makes mistakes. The key is learning from those mistakes so that we don't make the same ones twice.
See also Training

CONFORMATION

Good trail horses come in many shapes and sizes. Beauty lies in what the animal can do, not what scores it might garner in a show ring. A short-backed animal will ride rougher than a longer backed horse but can carry more weight for longer. I consider attitude, or disposition, over all other concerns. If you find a horse that clicks with you, check with your veterinarian to see how the animal will work in your program.
See also Animals – Factors to Consider in a Trail Horse

CONTAINMENT –TEMPORARY ELECTRIC FENCE

Electric fencing in the backcountry can provide a portable and cost-effective barrier that gives you nearly the same security, convenience, and reliability as at home.

Before electric fences, I spent several hours of each day in the backcountry monitoring the grazing of my animals. By monitoring, I mean hobbling then watching with an eagle eye while they ate and wandered, bringing them closer when warranted, and collecting them up when the grass over yonder became more tempting than what was under their noses. Failure to do so invariably meant a long walk to fetch my wandering herd. Now I relax by the camp stove with a cup of coffee while my mules relax, roll, and eat.

Electric fences are a psychological barrier that keeps our animals in and wild animals out. When a critter touches an electrified wire, the electricity passes through the animal, into the soil, to the ground rod, and back to the energizer. The electrical circuit is then completed, and the animal receives a harmless "correction" (a noticeably unpleasant shock) and becomes trained to stay clear of the fence.

Going electric took a few missteps before we settled on a solution that worked. Here's a backcountry electric fence system that works for us.

Parts of a Temporary Electric Fence:

Charger

The fence energizer is the heart of the system and a piece that I got wrong at first. I went with a 2 D-cell unit that sends out .04 joules of energy in my quest for lightweight solutions. While it worked fine at home, it wasn't nearly powerful enough in the less than perfect conditions you'll find at a campsite.

A different charger put out eight times the power (.35 joules), uses just 4 D-cells, and is used in commercial bear fences keeping grizzlies out of trouble. If it can keep a bruin out of camp, surely it will hold a few mules in. My theory is that I want to knock the socks off any critter that even considers breaching the fence. Go with the most powerful energizer you can, remembering that you'll rarely encounter perfect conditions when camping.

Electric Tape

You have a myriad of options on how to transmit your electric charge. The two most common are wire or tape. We started with a 9-strand wire because it rolls up into a small package, allowing me to carry more in a smaller space. That compact size turned out to be problematic as it wasn't easy to see. I ended up having to hang flagging tape on the wire. 1/2-inch-wide tape takes up a bit more room, but it's highly visible to everyone.

How much tape to bring depends on how big an enclosure you want to make. I've been with packers who fenced in several acres. I don't need nearly that much space and only haul 350 feet of tape. That gives me a corral of about eight thousand square feet that easily goes around my  highline area. I still take my animals out to graze beyond the enclosure, but I do this when it's convenient.

Posts

You need to hang the tape on something, and a few posts come in handy in the absence of trees. I took fiberglass posts and cut them in half. Then I glued on a ferrule as a joint between the segments so that the posts could break down and fit easily in a pack box.

When you're in camp, you can also use nearby trees as posts with insulators of bungee cords or even baling twine. Using nearby trees lets you considerably extend the size of the enclosure.

Ground

The biggest reason for electric fence failures is improper grounding. The electricity must complete a full circle back to the charger through the ground. The output pulse travels through the fence wire into the horse who is touching the wire, and then into the soil under the horse's hooves. The current then returns through the earth back to the ground system, which completes the circuit. Poor grounding gives weak shocks.

Good grounding depends on the surface where the fence is set up. Dry earth, sand, and gravel are poor conductors, substantially reducing the shock delivered by the fence. Electric fences work best on moist ground.

Electric Fence Miscellaneous bits and bobs:
Gate Handle and **Tape Reel**

Using an Electric Fence in the Backcountry

When I'm in a backcountry camp, I alternate between highlining, hobbling, and pasturing within the electric fenced area. I set up the electric fence around the highline. At night or if I leave camp without them, all my animals are on the highline. When I'm in camp, I'll let the ponies off the highline and let them graze and relax in their backcountry paddock while I cook or tinker around camp. Since my

setup is relatively small, I still take the mules out of their paddock to graze while hobbled, under my watchful eye.
See also Highline

CONTAINMENT – HIGHLINE

When you're ready to try camping with your horse a critical skill you should learn is how to set up a safe highline. A highline will keep your horse safe overnight and will help you get a good night's rest. For me, the highline is the gold standard.
See Highline

CONTAINMENT – PICKETING

Picket lines are another tool that can provide you with a way to graze your stock. A traditional picket line is made with a stake, a single leg hobble, and a long rope attaching both. The stake, or picket pin, should have a swivel so that as your animal walks around, it spins freely and doesn't create tangles. The rope should be thick and soft to reduce the chances of rope burns if it becomes wrapped around a leg. I've used 1½ inch cotton rope, about 30 feet long, for this purpose.

Training at home is paramount to ensure that your animals are comfortable with picketing before arriving at camp.

A benefit of picket training is that your animal will become better about giving to pressure and standing still if they get their foot caught in something like fence wire.

While picketing your animals is an option, I don't use this method. I've had too many critters get the rope wrapped around a leg. The wide diameter and the soft construction prevented rope burns, and their at-home training prevented an unwanted rodeo, but I'd rather not deal with the chances of either. For most of my trips, I'll either highline or use an electric fence.

CONTAINMENT – PORTABLE CORRALS

Horse camping is that special cherry on top of the beautiful pie that trail riding should be. A calm, quiet camp at the end of a day spent exploring trails far and wide is a beautiful thing. Falling asleep to the soft sounds of the horses eating and gently moving is part of the magic of horse camping.

Of course, the awful antithesis of this is waking with a start and discovering that the ponies have wandered away. It has happened to all of us.

Sweet dreams of trails traveled turn to nightmares in a heartbeat when the horses and mules vanish into the night. At best, it's lost sleep and the hassle of rounding them up. At worst, your trail partners may never be found.

I've always been a fan of highlines. Done well, these are fabulous for keeping our horses safe and near camp. But how to contain our mischievous mounts safely and securely if there are no handy trees? What if highlines aren't allowed?

The trailhead solution that I turn to when highlines aren't an option (and sometimes when they are) are safe and secure steel corral panels that let me get a good night's sleep without having to worry about my animals going on walk-about.

My corral panels are made of sturdy ¾ inch square steel tubing that holds up to rough treatment, holds my beasts, and store conveniently when not in use.

Steel vs. PVC – I choose steel panels because steel is a superior material to PVC. Steel is strong, lightweight when manufactured properly, and will not degrade in time due to UV radiation. Additionally, if there are problems, steel will bend. PVC is brittle and will shatter into sharp shards. Not something that I want my trail buddies to encounter. My 13, ¾ inch steel panels are also much easier to store than an equal number of 2" diameter PVC pipes.

What is portable? I've seen people with standard fence panels tied to the sides of their trailers, and my backcountry highline kit weighs under 3 pounds, so the portability of containment options varies.

For trailhead camping, I want the best combination of lightweight to set it up quickly, small size so I can easily transport it, and sturdy construction, so my animals stay put. It seems like many contradicting wants, but for me, these steel panels cover these bases nicely.

I prefer to reduce my workload as much as possible when horse camping. At under 20 pounds per panel, this system keeps me from working harder than I need to.

The panels hang securely over my trailer's wheel wells in transit with collapsible hangers.

With Ruger, my inquisitive troublemaker mule, I have found that I need to run a hot wire along the top rail to keep him from pushing the panels towards the always greener grass that is just out of reach. *See also Highline*

CONTOUR LINES – UNDERSTANDING TOPO MAPS

You probably already know that a compass and a paper map are part of the Ten Essentials. Learning to interpret that paper topo map (short for topographic map) is every bit as essential. Your map will tell a richly detailed story about the area you'll be exploring. We just have to open our eyes to see that story.

Have you ever looked closely at the squiggly lines scattered over your topo maps? Besides the obvious trails and rivers, the brown squiggly lines are contour lines. These fascinating lines represent the three-dimensional landscape of Earth within the two-dimensional space of a map. Contour lines give us 3-D glasses.

Contour lines are the map feature that make topographic trail maps useful for trip planning AND navigation in the field.

> PRO TIP
> ## Contour lines can never intersect or cross one another.
> Ink lines may blend together on a map, but contour lines can never touch in the real world.

What these unassuming lines do is plot the points of equal elevation on a map. If you were to trace the length of a contour line, each point would be the same height above sea level. If you were to walk the path of a contour line in real life, you would remain at the same elevation the entire time. You might be hanging from a cliff by your fingertips, but you would never go up or down.

How Contour Lines Describe Terrain

Simply put, contour lines indicate the steepness of the terrain. Where they're close together, elevation changes rapidly in a short distance; therefore, the terrain is steep. Where contour lines are far apart, the elevation changes slowly, indicating a gentle slope.

Common Terrain Features to Learn:

Contour lines indicate the shape of the terrain. Major terrain features that you'll encounter include peaks, valleys, saddles, and depressions. Each terrain feature has characteristic contour line patterns that make it easy to pick them out in the landscape.

Learning to identify the distinct features of common contour line patterns will help you read topo maps quickly, and recognize the various terrain features they represent in the real world.

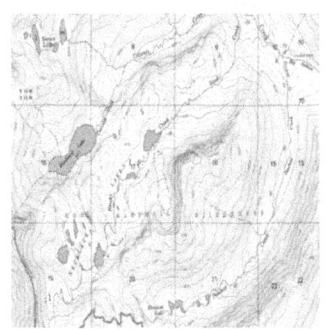 

PRO TIP
Most navigation and map reading is about matching the form of the terrain in front of you with that on the map.

Peak: A peak or hill is an area of high ground. From the top, the ground slopes down in all directions. Peaks are illustrated by contour lines forming concentric circles. The inside of the smallest closed circle is the top of the hill.

Valley: A valley is a stretched-out groove in the land, usually formed by a water feature, that has high ground on three sides. Valleys are illustrated by contour lines forming U-shaped or V-shaped patterns. The closed end of the contour line pattern (U or V) always points upstream or toward high ground.

Saddle: A saddle is a low point between two areas of higher ground. A saddle is illustrated by contour lines that typically look like an hourglass.

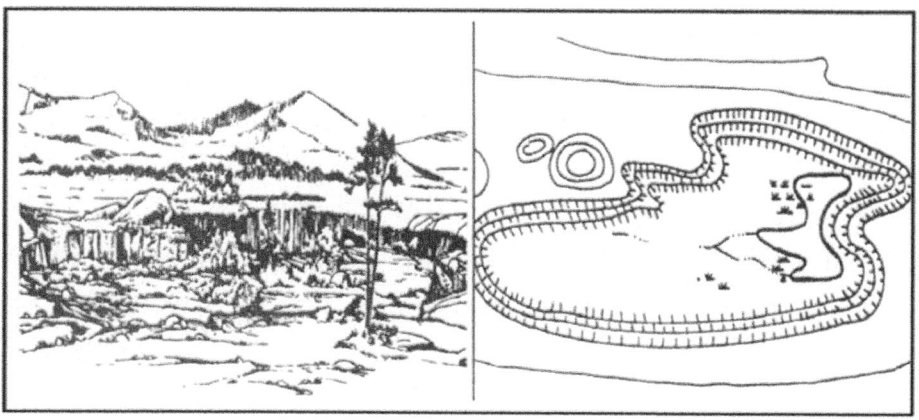

Depression: A depression is a low point on the ground. It could be described as simply a hole in the ground that isn't a lake. Depressions are represented by closed contour lines that have tick marks (hachure lines) pointing toward the low point.

Becoming proficient with reading contour lines takes practice. One of the easiest ways to do this is to always be aware of the shapes of the surrounding land, even when riding at your local park.

See also Maps, Navigation

COOKING - EQUIPMENT

An oft-quoted saying of Napoleon Bonaparte is that "An army marches on its stomach". This old adage is also relevant to horse riders and campers. After all, a great camp dinner is a beautiful flourish to a perfect day in the saddle. Let's discuss a few of the different ways to stay fed while camping with our mounts.

The Dutch oven, this thick-walled chunk of cast iron, has been around for hundreds of years for a good reason; they're excellent for wood-fired cooking and can produce a meal fit for royalty. The major downfall to a Dutch oven is its weight. At nearly 15 pounds for even a smallish oven, I don't envy the Lewis and Clark expedition, who hauled one across the continent during their Corps of Discovery Expedition. Modern forms of the venerable Dutch oven include significantly lighter aluminum versions. They're still heavy but less so than iron. The weight is the biggest reason why you'll most often find Dutch oven feasts at the trailhead and not so often in the backcountry, where a long-suffering mule has had to haul it in. If we ever meet while I'm trailhead camping, stop by for a bite. Chances are I'll have my Dutch oven on the fire, and spaghetti will be on the menu.

While a Dutch oven is faultless for trailhead cooking, the small size and negligible weight of modern backpacking stoves make them perfect for backcountry trips. In my opinion, there aren't many things better than a quiet breakfast while watching the animals graze in a remote meadow.

A small backpacker's stove is perfect for providing a cup of coffee and oatmeal for this type of repast. Weight and volume are my prime considerations when I venture into the backcountry without pack stock. To reduce the load as much as possible, I've found that single burner stoves work well for me. Feather-light and fitting in the palm of your hand, these stoves quickly produce the piping hot water needed for coffee and rehydrating freeze-dried fare.

I love a good campfire, and you might ask, "if weight is such a concern, why not just make a campfire and use that for cooking"? Unfortunately, campfires aren't always a viable option. Open fires are often illegal during the summer months when we're in the backcountry, and if fires are allowed, there are no guarantees that you'll be able to find dry wood. For peace of mind and a full stomach, a camp stove of some type is your best bet.

The classic and reliable Coleman Camp Stove is an in-between camp stove that works quite well when pack stock are part of the picture. These nearly indestructible workhorses allow for multi-course dishes in the grandest restaurant of all, the great outdoors.

My first and most memorable backcountry trip was with two long-time Back Country Horsemen of Washington members who introduced me to the world of camping with pack animals. The meal that I made by adding hot water to a plastic bag of "stuff" was  pleasant but in no way compared to the grand meal of steak, zucchini, onions, and green beans that were deftly prepared on a battered two-burner stove pulled from the depths of a pack mule's pannier bag. I'm eternally grateful not just that Russ and Ken shared their feast but more so that they introduced me to the experience of enjoying the backcountry with horses and mules.

CORRAL

Overnight campers will need some type of playpen for their ponies. Established campgrounds will often have these available for your use. Before turning the animals loose, check the corral for any hazards the previous tenants may have left. More than once, we've opted to highline the horses because the provided corrals weren't safe.
See also Containment, Highline

COWBOY

They were pragmatists, and you should be as well. Use the tack, gear, and equipment that work best for your intended purpose, not what looks cool in a western theme shop. E.g., That authentic western roping saddle is going to weigh down your already hard-working horse on the trail. Try a lightweight rig made for trail riding and take 20 or more pounds off your horse's load. Likewise, that good-looking oilskin duster is heavy, requires regular re-waxing, and will trip you when you're off your horse. A Gore-Tex jacket is much lighter and requires less maintenance.

CRUPPER

Very simply, a crupper is a piece of material that attaches to the rear of the saddle and loops around the base of your horse's tail to help secure and prevent the saddle from sliding forward.

It's best to introduce your animal to a crupper well before you arrive at the trailhead. When fitting the crupper, the strap should be snug enough that you can easily slide a couple of fingers between it and the base of your horse's tail. If it's too tight, your animal could very easily become annoyed or sored. If the crupper is too loose, it won't engage in time to stop your saddle from sliding forward.

One last note on cruppers. If you use one, you must keep it clean, very clean. A dirty crupper can, and will, sore the skin of your animal in short order.

Cruppers concentrate the pressure from the rider and saddle on a small area on the horse's tailbone. A more comfortable option for the horse would be a britchen.

See also Britchen

D

DECLINATION

On a map, north is easy to find (it's usually at the top). However, in the real world, magnetic north (where your compass needle points) and true north (on your map) can be considerably different: That difference is known as "declination".

Why Should You Care? A single degree of uncorrected declination could set you off course by 100 feet over a mile. In the U.S., declination varies from 20 degrees east in parts of the west coast to 20 degrees west in parts of the east

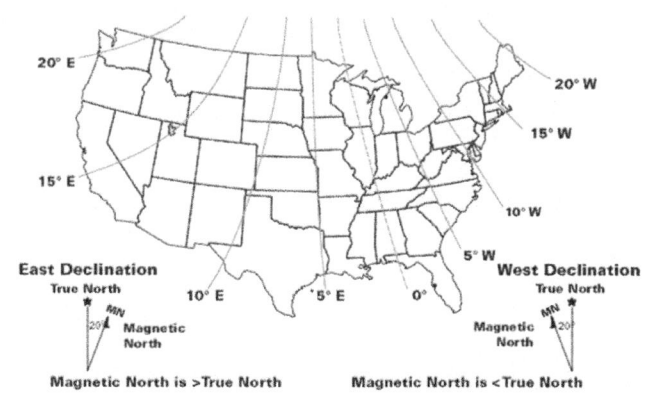

coast. Do the math. Twenty degrees times 100 feet, and you'll be off course by nearly four tenths of a mile before you have time to adjust your saddle. That's the difference between heading right or left at the next trail intersection. I think this illustrates why it's essential to adjust for declination. Failure to do so may make for an unplanned, very long day in the saddle.

Before you're able to adjust for it, you must find the declination value in your riding area. Topo maps generally list it, but the value varies over time. So, check the map's revision date and consult the National Oceanic and Atmospheric Administration (NOAA) website for the area's current magnetic declination.

Adjusting for declination varies with different compass models, and you'll need to read the instructions. Fortunately, after the declination is set for a trip, you don't have to think about it again until you travel to another area.

See also Compass, Navigation

PRO TIP
A better way to handle declination.

Draw magnetic north lines on your map and navigate using magnetic north.

DOGS

Dogs are truly man's best friend and a joy to be around. I've belonged to numerous canids throughout my life, and I have a soft spot for these most loyal of critters. Although I love my dogs, they don't accompany me on trail rides or venture out on wilderness trips with the horses.

Here are four reasons to keep fido home as well as what the dog must know if you insist on taking him out.

1 - To protect your dog from other animals

Sure, your pooch might be a descendant of the mighty wolf but allowing him to travel the trail off-leash exposes him to many threats. Predators often target domesticated animals. Coyotes, cougars, and others pose a danger to off-leash dogs. These predators are brash and often not fazed by a dog's size. Other less thought of, but equally real, hazards include porcupines and snakes. Keeping your dog at home also helps to avoid the risk of your dog triggering a predator (think bear) while off-leash before fleeing back to you with said predator close behind.

The animals your dog may encounter don't have to be wild to be a danger. There's also the issue of other domestic dogs, especially poorly trained ones wandering off-leash. The aftermath of two strange dogs getting into a rumble isn't pretty. Topping the list of trail dangers is our livestock. Untold numbers of dogs have encountered a horse, or mule, that wasn't keen on their attention and suffered for it. A well-aimed kick from a 1,000 lb. equine can make  for a very unpleasant trip to the emergency veterinarian.

2 - To protect your dog from trail hazards
Every year you'll find stories about dog rescues that could have been avoided had the animal simply been kept at home or on a leash. Natural spaces can pose risks to our less than wilderness savvy companions, from hidden mine shafts to cliffs, getting lost, and beyond. Keeping your dog on a leash or at home helps keep them away from these hazards that their canine brain may not fully understand as they follow their nose. Other trail and wilderness

hazards include various parasites and diseases, including giardia and plague.

3 - For the safety of other trail users

It seems that every dog owner thinks their dog "isn't aggressive". However, a dog doesn't have to be aggressive to be a problem. Many of the people that we share our trails with have well-founded fears of dogs. Your pup's bounding, happy, barky greeting may well be interpreted as aggression by a stranger. There are also instances of dogs running loose and causing accidents when they spooked another rider's horse.

4 - For the safety of the locals

When a dog spots native wildlife, there's a good chance they'll want to chase it. When this happens, it stresses out the native animal, something that itself may lead to death. Your dog's predatory behavior is normal. The chase drive is instinctual. The issue is that when prey animals are harassed, they use energy that they may need to survive. It's one thing for the locals to deal with each other; it's entirely another for us to bring our dogs into the mix and cause further problems. Loose dogs chasing wildlife is such an issue that most states have laws that penalize owners of these dogs.

These are the four main reasons my dog, Boo, doesn't accompany me on trail rides. That's not saying that Boo doesn't get out. We go on many hikes together where he stays safely on a leash and out of mischief, or go off-leash where legal when I can keep an eye on him without also having to control my horses and mules.

This isn't to say that there aren't dogs that are great as trail riding companions, just that there are a lot of things to consider.

What Dogs Need to Know Before They Hit the Trail

If you insist on bringing a canine companion with you on the trail, I suggest that your dog have an excellent grasp of these five basic commands first.

1) **Come** – A recall command should be the most important word in a dog's vocabulary. It's critically important on the trail because you don't know what distractions your dog will find.
2) **Stay** - You need to be able to stop your dog in his tracks. Your dog will encounter squirrels, rabbits, or other dogs. Without a solid stay, he may dart after an animal, unaware of other hazards.
3) **Leave it** – From dead animals to porcupines, a dog will always find items of interest on the trail. Items that you may not be as enthralled with.
4) **Go ahead** - It is much easier to stay focused on your horse and riding if fido stays in your line of sight ahead of you.
5) **Go behind** – Sometimes you'll want the dog following behind you at a safe distance.

Check the rules for the area that you're riding to be sure that off-leash dogs are allowed. Be painfully honest about your dog's abilities: If your dog listens to your voice only some of the time, they are not ready to accompany the ponies on the trail.

DUCT TAPE

This miracle material was created during WWII when the military needed a strong, flexible, and waterproof tape for field repairs. If it can't be fixed with duct tape, all is lost. A length wrapped around a pencil is handy for mending many of the broken things you'll encounter and is small enough to easily stash in your saddlebags.

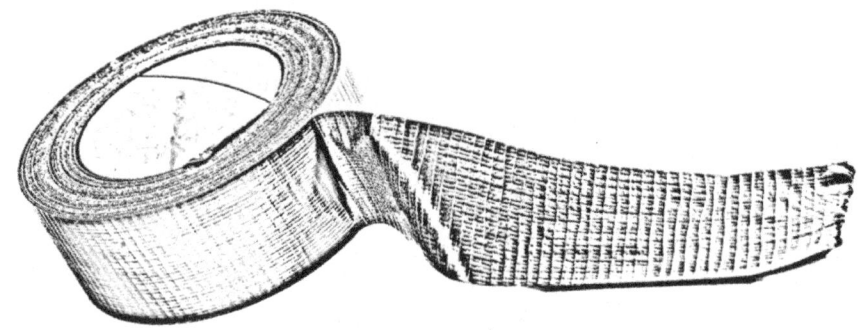

Six Uses for Duct Tape

1) Patch material - Don't let a damaged tent ruin your camping trip! Use a few pieces of duct tape to patch up tears in the fabric of your tent. You can also use duct tape to temporarily fix a broken tent pole until a replacement is sorted out.

2) First aid - One of the reasons why duct tape is so useful is because it's so sticky! If you've got a painful blister that's rubbing against your clothing or gear, cover it with a small square of duct tape to reduce irritation. As an improvised band-aid for covering a cut (human or animal), apply a small amount of anti-bacterial ointment to a cotton ball and secure the cotton ball over the cut with duct tape. Lastly, you can even remove a sliver close to the skin's surface by applying duct tape tight and letting it sit for a minute. Remove the duct tape slowly to pull the sliver out.

3) Reseal packages - A quick and simple trick: Keep food fresh by resealing bags and cans with a layer or two of tape.

4) Build shelter - You can make a shelter in a pinch if you have a tarp and duct tape. First, make grommets in the tarp by puncturing the plastic using your knife or a sharp stick. Then, reinforce the hole on both sides with duct tape. Make rope with duct tape (see tip #5 below) and string them through the grommets. Then get creative with your tarp-building skills and use trees, branches, rocks, and logs as anchor points.

5) Make rope - If you discover that you're missing a rope, you can easily make your own. Take about a 4-foot-long strip of duct tape and tear it down the middle to make two strips. Attach the two strips end-to-end to make an 8-foot-long strip with the sticky side facing the same direction. Circle one end of the strip around a water bottle (or other similar-sized objects, like a log or rock) and stick it back to itself; you'll be able to suspend the water bottle in the loop you've created. Have a friend hold the other end of the tape and spin the bottle around and around to twist the cord tight.

6) Use as a fire starter - Duct tape is surprisingly flammable. In a pinch, it could be the secret tool to get a campfire going. For an even more reliable fire starter, wrap duct tape around a bundle of dryer lint to create a flammable tootsie roll.

See also Emergency, Essentials

E

EASY DEWORMING

Deworming used to be an ordeal that neither the horses nor I enjoyed. I would sneak up to the horse, grab the halter tight, and jam the dewormer tube in his mouth. It was a vain attempt to get the job done quickly before the inevitable fight. Not only did this make the horse defensive, but it also made the process downright dangerous. Deworming days were dreaded by all involved. It doesn't have to be.

I now look at deworming as an ongoing process, not an event to be avoided. If you take the time to make administering oral medications a regular part of your routine, the process can become much more manageable and worry-free. My goal is for deworming to be a casual kind of event. No worries, no fuss, and most importantly, no drama. Here's how I get my animals to relax and accept their meds.

1 - Accept the Tube
The first step is getting the horse used to having the tube around him. I rub an empty applicator all over him. If he fights it, I hold the tube on him until he stops resisting then I take it away. Approach and retreat are key here. As soon as the horse stops moving, I remove the tube. I've had horses where at first, I couldn't even approach them with the tube. In those cases, I start by just standing near them and then slowly progress to touching them. Take your time and be relaxed.

2 – Add the Sweet Stuff
Once your horse can tolerate having an empty tube resting on his face without any fuss, it's time to up the ante and ask him to take the tube

in his mouth. It helps to have the tube filled with something good. I like using applesauce. Fill an empty dewormer, or a similar type of tube, with applesauce. Don't bother wiping off any residue. Gently place the tube near the horse's mouth so he can smell and taste the applesauce on the outside. Once the horse learns that the tube contains something yummy, you'll be able to gently depress the plunger and squirt the contents into his mouth. Repeat this practice "deworming" with the good stuff until the process is smooth and easy. When my horses see a deworming tube now, they come running for their treat.

3 – Deworm

Once your animals are excited and happy when they see the

deworming tube, it's time to use something that reduces internal parasites better than applesauce. Now is the time to use a little deception and then a lot of apologies. Before heading out with a real dewormer, I smear the outside with applesauce and fill an empty tube with applesauce. The coating on the outside of the real dewormer will help disguise the foul smell and taste until it's too late, and the applesauce-filled tube serves as an apology. Always end on a positive note. If you administer the nasty medication and finish the process there, your horse will remember it longer than you.

4 - Return to the Sweet Stuff

To reinforce the idea that 99.9% of the time a dewormer tube is a good thing, I follow up with applesauce shots for the next few days after applying a real dewormer. Until once again, the ponies come running when they see the tubes. Once a month, I break out the applesauce tubes to keep the good vibes going.

I rely on my horses and mules to get me into wild and fabulous places. Part of preparing them for that requires regular preventive medical care, including deworming. Talk with your vet about what type of dewormer and when to use it. I want my animals to trust me. I work towards that goal by making what used to be an unpleasant experience something to be enjoyed.

ELECTRIC FENCE
See also Containment

EMERGENCY
Are you prepared in case something goes wrong on a trail ride or a camping trip? 99.8% of rides and trips will be uneventful with no misadventures. It's that .2% that can be awkward. Being prepared goes beyond having well-trained horses and mules.
Are you ready to spend an unplanned night on the trail if all goes south? Are you prepared to act as an emergency doctor or veterinarian until you get to a real doc?
See also Essentials, First Aid, Training

EMERGENCY PLAN

Creating a trail ride plan and leaving it with friends or family is a safety basic and an excellent habit to cultivate. It prevents unnecessary anxiety and, in an emergency, saves precious time for search and rescue responders.

Discuss and leave a copy of the plan with someone reliable, responsible, and who knows how, when, and why to contact authorities.

Ride Emergency Plan
From: www.TrailMeister.com – Your return to ride guide

If you have not heard from me by (time) _____ of (day) _____ of (month) _____, please contact search and rescue at 911 and report me as overdue. Provide search and rescue with ALL of the information below.

Time/date of Departure: _____   Expected Time/date of Return: _____

Names (include your own)	Age	Phone#	Physical Description	Medical issues / medications

Emergency Equipment Carried: ☐ - 1st Aid Kit ☐ - Flashlight ☐ - Map ☐ - Compass ☐ - Knife ☐ - Water ☐ - Food ☐ - Communications ☐ - Lighter/matches ☐ - Rain gear ☐ - Medications
Other: _____

Vehicle / Trailer	Make	Color	License #

Equine	Sex	Description	Age	Breed	Shod	Brands

Veterinarian: _____   Vet Contact info: _____
Farrier: _____   Farrier Contact info: _____
In Case of Emergency (ICE) – Name- Relationship – Contact information: _____

Trip Details: Activity Type: ☐ day ride ☐ camping

Trailhead Name: _____ State: ___ Address / Coordinates: _____
Planned Trails and Route: _____

Backup Plan: _____

Additional Trip Notes: _____

Free Emergency Planning Statement – from www.TrailMeister.com – World's Largest Horse Trail and Camp Guide

If your plans change, contact the person with whom you left the plan! You don't want a search and rescue team sent for you if not needed.

The more information you leave behind, the better prepared your loved ones will be when and if they need to notify an emergency response team. A thorough plan will assist the search and rescue teams that may be helping you.

https://www.trailmeister.com/trail-ride-itinerary/

PRO TIP

Research, document, and distribute your plan before you leave.

EQUITATION

Equitation is the art or practice of horse riding or horsemanship. More specifically, equitation may refer to a rider's position while mounted and encompasses a rider's ability to ride correctly and with effective aids.

All too often, trail riders become complacent. After all, it's "just a trail ride", or "it's just a trail horse".

No, it is not. What we as trail riders and horse campers ask of ourselves and our animals far surpasses that of most arena riders.

The heart of equitation is forming a relationship between horse and rider so that the two work in tandem as a team.

ESSENTIALS - THE 11 ESSENTIALS

Back in the early 1930s, a group of mountaineers in the Pacific Northwest created the 10 Essentials; a list of items intended to:

A. To help you respond positively in an accident or emergency.
B. To help you safely spend an unplanned night outside.

Over time, the 10 Essentials have evolved from a list of individual pieces to a list of practical systems. You probably won't need every item on every ride, but these essential items could be a lifesaver in an emergency.

Most forward-thinking trail riders already take along a few things in case of an emergency. This checklist will help you remember what to bring.

The Trail Rider's 10 Essentials and a bonus essential!

1 - Navigation

Can every member of your party determine where they are and find a way back to the trailhead?

Modern trail riders have various navigation tools available to help them "Stay Found". A prepared rider carries and knows how to use these three navigation tools: map, compass, and GPS device. These tools will help identify where you are and distance to your destination. They can also help find campsites, water, or an alternate route.

2 - Illumination

For horse riders, headlamps are the flashlight of choice, freeing your hands for all sorts of tasks, from untacking a horse to starting a fire. In case of a longer-than-planned ride, a headlamp will provide welcome illumination. Modern,

efficient, and bright LEDs have virtually replaced incandescent bulbs. An LED bulb will last seemingly forever, but batteries don't so carry spares.

3 - First Aid Supplies

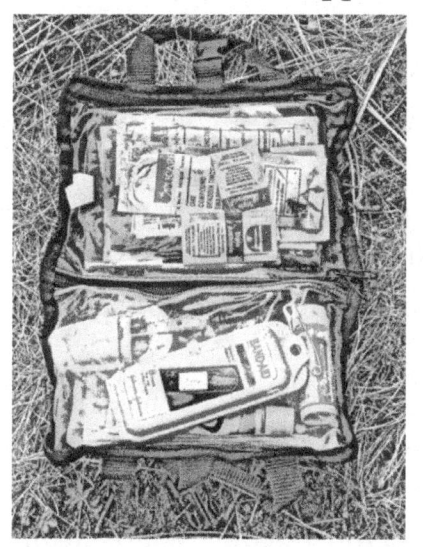 Carry a 1st Aid kit and increase your kit's effectiveness with the knowledge to use it: take a first-aid class. On the trail and in the mountains, trained emergency responders may be hours or even days away.

Pre-assembled first-aid kits take the guesswork out of building your own, though most people personalize their kits to suit individual needs. Any kit should include treatments for blisters, adhesive bandages of various sizes, gauze pads, adhesive tape, disinfecting ointment, and over-the-counter pain medication. For a longer-term ride or backcountry pack trip, talk to your physician about appropriate prescription medications. Carrying a 1st Aid kit, and knowing how to use it, can help make a bad situation much more bearable.

4 - Repair Kit

Knives and multi-purpose tools are helpful in first aid, food preparation, and repairs. Every rider needs to carry one. From repairing broken tack on the trail to making bandages and removing splinters, having a way to repair equipment on the trail will help keep a ride on track.

Other repair kit supplies carried by nearly every trail rider include duct tape and baler twine. These all-purpose fix-it items have saved many rides! Think about the length and nature of each ride in

deciding what to add to your repair kit. Other tools such as pliers and repair items, including needle and thread, cable ties, cordage, and replacement parts for equipment such as a water filter, have a place in every horse camper's gear list.

5 - Communications

Historically, horsemen have needed to be self-reliant, and riders should still have that mindset today. However, when an emergency unfolds despite preparation and training, most people will welcome help. A reliable communications system could provide that support.

Satellite Messengers and Personal Locator Beacons determine your position using GPS technology and communicate via satellites. These tools have saved many lives, and every trail rider should strongly consider carrying one. Satellite communication devices are reliable in remote areas. Regular cell phones, which rely on your proximity to cell towers, are not. Unless you are positive that you'll have a dependable connection, assume that your phone won't function.

6 - Fire

Can you reliably start and maintain a fire? Its heat and light will make a world of difference on a cold night spent outside. For many people, a disposable butane lighter works fine. Matches are also suitable so long as they are stored in a waterproof container.

More experienced outdoors people use ferrocerium fire strikers that create intense showers of sparks to start fires in the worst of conditions.
See also Fire Making

7 - Emergency Shelter

If you're really in a bind, you might be waiting for rescue. Anything that will protect you from the elements will be appreciated in such a situation. Tarps, emergency blankets, or even large garbage bags provide a way to protect yourself, or others, from the cold, wind, rain, or sun. Emergency "space blankets" are a cheap, lightweight, and compact tool that can help if you get stranded or injured on the trail.

8 - Insulation

Are you prepared in case the weather changes? We've all been caught in an unscheduled rain shower. It wasn't pleasant. Conditions can abruptly turn wet, windy, or cold on the trail, or an injury may result in an unplanned night out. Hypothermia can be a serious concern even in the summer if you're stuck outside overnight.

9 - Hydration

Humans are 60% water, and we're constantly losing it. Without enough water, your body's muscles and organs can't function as intended. Always carry at least one water bottle or hydration bladder.

Wide-mouth containers are easy to refill. Always start a ride with a full container and have the skills and tools required to obtain and purify additional water if necessary.

10 - Nutrition

I'm always glad to find an extra snack in the bottom of my saddlebags. Extra food helps keep up your energy and morale. Carry extra high-calorie, nutrient-dense food that lasts a long time, requires no cooking and is easily digestible. Combinations of jerky, nuts, candy, and granola work well. If you're a dedicated coffee drinker, a few packets of instant will provide a caffeine fix.

Bonus Essential - Common Sense

The 11th and most important essential. Having the right gear is one thing; knowing how and when to use it is quite another. Often, it's not a person's equipment that saves them. It's their experience, know-how, and good judgment. Inexperience, or a lack of good judgment, is what gets people into trouble. We must develop the knowledge to use our tools effectively. Grow skills beyond horsemanship; it'll make for much better trail riding and horse camping trips.

ETIQUETTE ON THE TRAIL

Here are a few words that go together, peanut butter and jelly, horses and trails, etiquette and safety.

- Etiquette: noun: the rules governing the proper way to behave.
- Safety: noun: the condition of being safe from undergoing or causing hurt, injury, or loss.

We can all use a refresher regarding trail etiquette, this is not just for the sake of Miss Manners but also to help keep you and me out of harm's way. Etiquette and safety are partners on the trail. The breach of one can easily create a lack of the other.

Some of the more universal safety rules that most of us already know and follow are easy to remember but still bear repeating.

- Carry emergency gear on your body (not on your mount).
- Carry a trail map and know how to read it.
- Pack a first aid kit.
- Maintain a safe distance between animals in a group.
- In a group, ride at the speed and level of the least experienced rider.
- Ask before speeding up.
- Make sure that you and your animals are ready for the trail. Muscles, endurance, and skills are built gradually.
- Desensitize your horse well in advance of a trail trip.

Here are a few etiquette items that every rider should keep in mind.

Multi-Use Means Multiple Users - In most parts of the country, trails are open to and shared by equestrians, hikers, and bicycle riders, among others. Sharing the trail can and does work when people respect each other and work cooperatively.

Before you load the trailer always check to see what types of travelers you'll be sharing the trail with. If hikers, bikers, or off-road vehicles (ORVs) are allowed, be prepared for those encounters.

It is important to remember that some people have not had the luxury of your experience with stock and may not know how to act around equines. With a friendly approach, these meetings can be an opportunity to inform and educate other trail users. Education with friendly respect greatly reduces bad trail encounters for everyone.

Yield With Common Sense - Although the convention for trail rights of way is that both bikers and hikers make way for horsemen, temper this with common courtesy and common sense. If the approaching hiker/biker party is struggling or has fewer options to "pull over," be courteous and let them pass by, regardless of who might technically have trail priority.

Uphill Travel is Hard, Don't Make it Worse - Traveling uphill is a lot of work for horses, hikers, and bikers. The self-propelled crowd is usually focused downward and trying not to lose any of the precious momentum they need to make the climb. Make it easier on these poor souls by letting them make the call about stopping or continuing their slow plod.

Leave No Trace is More Than You Remember - Leave No Trace (LNT) is more than just picking up after yourself. There are seven central tenets of the LNT movement, and all of them apply to stock users.

- Plan Ahead – A little preparation will save a lot of hassle later. Look into the area, contact the local land manager, and check the weather before you load the trailer.

- Travel on Durable Surfaces – If it's a muddy mess, find a drier trail.
- Dispose of Waste Properly – If you packed it in, pack it out.
- Leave What you Find – Trail treasures are cool. Give the next adventurer the same thrill by leaving what you found where you found it.
- Minimize Campfire Impacts – Pay attention to fire bans and reuse existing fire rings.
- Keep Wildlife Wild – Follow bear-wise practices, and if you travel with your dog, don't let it hassle the natives.
- Say Hello - When you run across other trail users, stop and chat. It's about more than just being friendly; it's about safety and making people equate equines with positive experiences.

These are just a few examples of safety and etiquette notions that we should keep in mind while we're on the trail. Remember that although you'll follow these common-sense guidelines, others may not.

Don't Let the Rogues Get You Down – You may encounter people that haven't learned simple trail etiquette. You may run into people that feel they have a right to do whatever they want, whenever they want. They are the dregs that make the worst impressions. Keep both eyes open for them for your safety and recognize the many more polite, courteous, and enjoyable people that you'll encounter.

BOB
MARSHALL
WILDERNESS
HELENA-
EWIS & CLARK
National
Forest

F

FEAR IN THE SADDLE

If you ride a horse, you've experienced fear. Whether in an arena or on the trails, the potential for problems is real. Our job as riders is not to try to put aside our trepidation; in large part, our fears are legitimate. If we learn to understand those fears and find ways to minimize the inherent danger of our equestrian activities, we'll be much better riders and have a much better time on the trail.

Anticipating the "what ifs" of an adventurous trail ride will help you prepare for any eventualities that may occur. By mentally preparing yourself ahead of time, you'll find that the backcountry's mountains and valleys are much less intimidating.

Here are a few tips to help, whether you're in the backcountry, the front country, or anywhere in between.

- Relax. Yes, this is much easier said than done. When you're tense, your horse knows it, and your riding suffers. If you can get your body to relax, it will help you feel more relaxed emotionally.

- Breathe. When you're tense, you unconsciously hold your breath. To start breathing regularly, try talking or singing; when I get anxious, you'll often hear me singing. Badly. You may not win a Grammy Award, but you will feel much better.

- Balance. When you're tense, you tend to lean forward into a fetal position. Fight this by sitting up straight and deep in the saddle, putting your shoulders back (I tell my students to sit tall like a Marine). You'll soon feel how much easier it is to breathe, and sing, and relax.

- Positive. Find something to focus on that's optimistic. Think about how much fun it is to ride with your favorite trail buddy. Fear could ruin a great ride, but you can overcome this by focusing on all the wonderful circumstances that have led to you being in the saddle and on the trail.

See also Confidence

FEED

Feed for our hard-working trail horses is an important consideration. With their delicate digestive systems, we want to reduce stress as much as possible while camping, and that includes thinking about their feed.

What type of feed, how much should you take, and what are some of the rules and regulations where you're going?

Try to keep your feeding routine as similar as possible to what they're used to at home. When this isn't an option, start them on their new rations at least a week before your trip. Slowly increase the ratio of new to old.

One example of when you definitely won't be able to keep their usual feed is when you're wilderness camping. Chances are you won't be able to pack in hay and that your animals will be grazing for their meals. If your horse doesn't typically have access to pasture at home, you'll want to introduce pasture well before your trip. The sudden introduction of fresh grass, if not accustomed, could lead to gastrointestinal distress, diarrhea, and colic.

Take extra feed. When you're planning meals, take more than you think you'll need. You may stay a day longer. You may want to feed a little extra. Running out of feed is never a good thing, so bring two or more extra days' worth, just in case you need it.
See also Grazing in the Backcountry, Weed Free

FIRE MAKING

Let's face it, campfires are good and proof that God loves us and wants us to be happy. When it's been pouring rain for several days, you've got one match left, and you're desperate to get the campfire blazing, having a good fire starter to help get things going can be comforting.

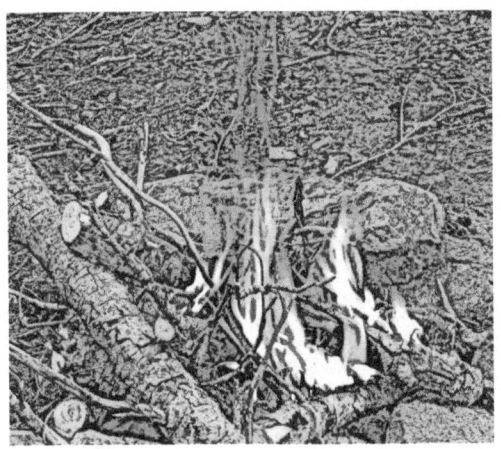

From dryer lint to pinecones and cotton balls, it's easy to make fire starters. DIY fire starters are one of the few guarantees in life. They're certain to make your fire starting struggles a thing of the past. Inexpensive and easy to make, they're all about reducing your fire-starting stress.

Here are some of my favorites:

Dryer Lint & Egg Cartons

The classic DIY fire starter is a wad of dryer lint placed in the empty well of a cardboard egg carton with melted wax poured over it. It's an easy project and brings back memories of grade school arts and crafts.

Cotton Balls & Petroleum Jelly

When petroleum jelly is worked into the ball, they're lightweight and are highly flammable, if a bit messy. I store mine in an old Altoids tin stashed in my saddlebags.

Hand Sanitizer

Squeeze a glob of hand sanitizer on kindling, and it will burn long enough to dry it out. Make sure the product you are using contains alcohol. Some companies are now making alcohol-free sanitizer, and that won't work.

Waxed Paper & Dryer Lint

Waxed paper burns well on its own. You can also wrap dryer lint or sawdust in the paper, twisting both ends to hold the contents. It's a flammable tootsie roll.

Chips

The greasier, the better when choosing which snacking chip will burn the best. Trust me, they do burn. Pringles and Fritos are my choices. Once the fire is going, it's snack time.

Duct Tape

Yes, one more trick for working with duct tape. It's highly flammable and burns for a good chunk of time. I wrap pieces of duct tape around my lighter and water bottle, so it's always on hand. Sometimes I'll even squeeze some hand sanitizer on it as well, to get things going.

Rubber Tubing

It's probably the most toxic fire starter on the list, but it's effective. Keep the old bicycle tube and cut it into strips. Just don't breathe in the fumes when it's ignited.

Cotton Pads in Wax

My favorite fire starter. These are waterproof and don't take up much space. Simply dip cotton makeup pads in melted wax, then set them aside to harden and dry. These are less messy than the cotton ball and petroleum jelly trick and are much easier to store.

Melting Wax Caution

You can melt wax without burning down the house. Wax is highly flammable, so don't throw a cube of it in a pot and heat directly over a stove burner. Slow down the melting rate and reduce the chance of combustion by using a double boiler system. Place the container with the wax inside a pot of hot water. The simmering water will melt the wax at a slower and safer rate. Melted wax is a real mess to clean up, so you may wish to use an old can rather than a cooking pot to melt the wax.

FIRST AID KIT

Are you prepared to be a doctor (Veterinarian or MD) long enough to manage a minor injury or stabilize a more serious wound? In such situations, a well-stocked and accessible emergency first-aid kit is indispensable.

> PRO TIP
>
> **It's not just the items you carry but rather it's having the knowledge to use those items.**

Be prepared to stabilize any injuries your horse incurs until your veterinarian arrives by maintaining a conveniently located equine first-aid kit. I have three different first aid kits: Barn kit – Trailer kit – Trail kit; I stock each kit with the items I'll need until the veterinarian arrives. Time is critical when an accident happens, and you don't want to waste time hunting around for bandages, a thermometer, or other necessities.

Over the years, I've compiled a list of items to include in our first-aid kit.

Basic 1st Aid Equipment

- A tight-sealing plastic container. Whatever you choose, make sure it's clean, airtight, and waterproof to ensure the contents stay sterile and ready to use. The container serves to hold the kit and as a bucket to soak hooves or wash a wound.
- Headlamp (with working batteries) to care for your horse on a dark night or dimly lit barn.
- Rectal thermometer—a plastic digital version is safer than the old school glass types.
- Small jar of petroleum jelly or other lubricant to help insert a thermometer.
- Stethoscope to check heart rate and listen to gut sounds.
- Surgical gloves to help prevent wound contamination.
- Roll of duct tape—convenient to wrap a hoof because it is waterproof and durable.
- Safety scissors with rounded ends to avoid cutting your horse.
- Tweezers—handy to help remove a splinter or ticks.
- Wire cutters to free a horse from wire.
- Sharp knife to use if a horse is tangled in ropes or has a foot stuck in a hay net.
- Cold pack to reduce swelling from an injury. Chemical cold packs that create "instant cold" are handy when ice or cold hosing isn't available.
- First-aid knowledge book.

Treatment Supplies - Horses can suffer a variety of injuries. Whether or not the situation requires an emergency call to your veterinarian or is something you may be able to treat yourself at home, you'll want supplies to quickly and gently clean and disinfect any wound.

They include:
- Antiseptic scrub such as Betadine (povidone-iodine) or Nolvasan (chlorhexidine) for washing/disinfecting a wound.
- Antiseptic wound cream, powder, or spray-on treatment to prevent infection and encourage healing – always seek veterinary advice before applying these products.
- Saline solution with a squirt nozzle - for flushing hard-to-reach, delicate wounds, such as near an eye.
- Triple-antibiotic ointment to treat minor cuts, scrapes, or burns.
- Electrolyte paste for treating dehydration.

Bandages

Once a wound has been cleaned, you'll need various bandaging materials to cover and keep it clean. You also want them on hand to stop bleeding quickly. Bandaging items include:
- Nonstick sterile gauze pads (telfa) squares to clean and cover small wounds.
- Self-sticking bandages— such as Vetrap™— to keep the gauze squares in place. Replace these annually.
- Gauze rolls for padding.
- Sanitary napkins or diapers – non-sterile wound dressings.

Medications

Depending on your veterinarian's comfort level with your skills, you may want to have prescription medications in your 1st Aid Kits. Ask your veterinarian to teach you when and in what circumstances to administer these drugs. If it is at all possible, always consult with your veterinarian first. If they can get to your horse quickly, they might not want you to administer anything, so they have a clearer idea of the extent of the issue.

Phenylbutazone ("bute") and flunixin meglumine (Banamine) are prescription nonsteroidal anti-inflammatory pain relievers. Talk with your veterinarian to learn the correct dosages and when to use them.

No matter how extensive your first-aid kit is, it will never replace a call to your veterinarian in an emergency. Your veterinarian has years of experience and skills that you don't possess. We just  need the skills to stabilize any injuries the horse incurs until a veterinarian can examine the animal.

6 Things to Do Before an Emergency Happens

- Have your veterinarian and farrier's contact information in all your 1st Aid Kits, save it in your phone, and post it in your barn.
- Know how to take your horse's temperature, pulse, and respiration and be aware of these typical resting vital signs. Ask your veterinarian to teach you how. Write down these figures so you can tell the veterinarian your animals' baseline numbers.

- Check your first-aid kit regularly (I check mine annually). Discard and replace expired medications and supplies.
- Replace anything you take out of your 1st Aid kit as soon as possible.
- Educate yourself. Make sure you know how to use everything in your kit, or have your veterinarian show you. Practice how to wrap your horse's leg before a stressful emergency.
- Keep your horse's health records up to date and handy, so you can answer any questions your veterinarian might have about his medical history. This is especially important when you travel.

See also Essentials

FIRST AID KNOWLEDGE

Having the knowledge to use your first aid kit, and improvise if needed, is just as important as carrying the gear. We talk to great lengths about providing care for our horses and mules in case a ride becomes "eventful". But we all too often neglect the human component of trail riding and camping with horses. Our human bodies are also prone to injuries, trauma, and illness. Worse, we don't know when an injury may happen to us, the people we love, or those around us. Can you honestly say, right now, that you have the skills to care for an injured person competently?

> PRO TIP
>
> *Being able to administer first aid / CPR is one of the most important skills anyone can have. Learn the basics of first aid and keep these skills fresh. Your friends and family are worth it.*

It's always good to have some basic knowledge to handle life's emergencies. Be able to keep the situation from going from bad to worse, or until medical help arrives.

Here are the most common responses when I ask if people have 1st aid training at my trail riding clinics.

- Too busy – Really?
- Don't know where to go for a class – Google it.
- Already have enough knowledge – No, you don't.
- Accidents happen to other people, not to them or their friends and family. Are you willing to bet your friend's and family's lives on it?

I think we can agree that all the above excuses are weak.

Here are five good reasons to learn 1st Aid and be the trail riding partner your friends and family deserve.

- Create confidence - Possessing basic 1st Aid knowledge means you'll be more confident in your skills and abilities. Taking first aid training will give you the confidence to help someone in need. The people around you will feel safer and more secure knowing that you'll be able to help them if the trip becomes "interesting".
- Prevent situations from becoming worse - In some cases, when a person doesn't receive basic 1st Aid care straightaway, their condition could deteriorate rapidly. By being able to provide basic care, you may be able to stabilize the victim until help arrives. You'll learn how to improvise if a first aid kit is not

available, meaning that you'll be able to cope with many situations.

- Increase safety - The basis of first aid training is "prevention". It is always better to be safe than to be sorry. The knowledge of 1st Aid prompts people to be more alert and safer in their surroundings.

- Increase comfort - Not all accidents necessitate a trip to the hospital, but it doesn't mean they don't cause some amount of pain. By knowing how to act, even by employing simple techniques such as applying an ice pack correctly, you'll help relieve the patient's discomfort. You'll also provide emotional support by remaining calm and collected, making the patient feel more secure.

- Help save lives - It's a fact that having first aid training helps save lives. That's not all; giving appropriate 1st Aid can help reduce a person's recovery. Your friends and family are worth it.

A comprehensive 1st Aid training course will help prepare you for a wide range of situations and give you the confidence and knowledge to deal with them quickly, correctly, and efficiently. Please take the first step towards becoming 1st Aid trained. Thank you.

FITNESS

The rigors of riding affect not just our mounts but also us as riders. Not only should we gradually work our horses into shape and keep them in condition, but we should also get ourselves in the best shape possible to withstand the physicality of trail riding.

FLASHLIGHT

Flashlights are extremely useful outdoors and make for a much more enjoyable and safer camping experience. I prefer headlamp versions that free my hands.

See also Essentials

PRO TIP

Look for lights with switches that won't turn on accidentally.

FLORA AND FAUNA

The great counterweight to the lure of the outdoors is the fear of the unknown. What if the weather turns for the worse? What if my horse acts up? What if I become lunch for a grizzly?

Here's the hard truth. Most people spend entirely too much time and energy worrying about menacing — but low-chance threats like bears, cougars, wolves, and not nearly enough thought concerning themselves with the dull and common dangers such as bees, blisters,  and hypothermia. To confirm this theory, take a quick test. How many times have you been mauled by a bear or a mountain lion? Now compare that figure with the number of times you've encountered bad weather, dealt with an unruly horse, or encountered bees on a ride.

One reason riders and campers worry about the wrong things is largely because of the media and writers like me. Adding the phrase "When Grizzlies Attack!" to a title sells more magazine copies, even if your chance of having a stand-off with a bear is much less than that of having a winning lotto ticket magically appear in your saddlebags. I'm not suggesting that you ignore potential threats like bears, wolves, and cats, but to drop them a few rungs down the worry ladder. If you're riding or camping in an active bear area, take sensible precautions such as carrying bear spray, making noise, bear-bagging your food, and avoiding huckleberry thickets. But don't fixate so much on these critters that you spook at every rustle of leaves, or even worse, fail to enjoy the ride and the trip. It all comes back to the most important outdoor skill everyone should practice, common sense.

Ignoring the hysteria can be hard to do and less than exciting. On rides with my wife, I've been guilty of pointing into the forest and reminding her that there are undoubtedly creatures watching us as they skulk in the darkness. For some reason, Celeste doesn't seem to appreciate my wickedly keen sense of observation. Here are a few words to the wise. Firstly, don't alarm your wife, husband, riding partner, or others with tall tales of the abundance of apex predators. Secondly, prioritize your outdoor concerns with the help of the following two lists.

1. Pay More Attention to These...
- Ensure that you and your animals are in shape and condition for trail riding. 610,000 people die each year from heart disease. When I get off and walk it's because I need some exercise, not because I'm having a moment.
- Desensitize your horse to scary situations you may encounter on the trail, such as hikers and bicycles, in a safe environment, such as an arena.
- Keep bugs away by applying insect repellant. According to the World Health Organization, in 2016 there were 94 deaths from the mosquito-borne West Nile Virus. Over 600,000 people die each year after being bitten by mosquitoes bearing the deadly malaria parasite.

- The non-human creatures that cause more American deaths than any other are bees and wasps. In a typical year, nearly 100 US deaths are caused by bee stings. This number is probably underestimated, as some bee sting deaths are erroneously attributed to heart attacks, sunstroke, and other causes.
- Wear a helmet. Using data from the National Trauma Databank between 2003 and 2012, researchers found that equestrian sports contributed to the highest percentage of traumatic brain injuries (TBI) for adults.

2. Worry Less About These…
- Bears – Black and grizzly bears have been responsible for 48 fatalities over the past 20 years. Compare that to the 40,200 traffic deaths recorded in 2016 alone.
- Wolves – These wild canids are much less lethal than man's best "friend". Domestic dogs kill 30-40 people annually. Since 1900 wolves have been responsible for a total of 4 deaths in North America.
- Mountain Lions / Cougars – There have been 25 cougar fatalities in the one hundred and twenty-seven years since records have been kept on the subject. Compare that to the 262 rodent spread hantavirus deaths from 1993 to 2020.

G

GADGETS

Amongst horse riders and especially horse campers, including trailhead and backcountry persuasions, one topic consistently sparks debate: ropework or gadgets?

Are you a knot purist who sees hardware devices as redundant, a waste of time and weight, or are you a knot-averse rider who avoids knots like the plague?

Each of these groups has very valid points and, in all practicality, none of them are right or wrong. While I'm a fan of knots, I also find a fair number of hardware devices quite useful.

Considering Gadgets and Hardware

Hardware solutions can be helpful. They can reduce the time required to set up camp. Hardware can also fail. I think that anyone working with horses and mules should have at least a basic understanding of the knots listed in the pages ahead for when hardware devices fail and improvisation becomes a necessity.

I have a few criteria for "good" hardware:

- The main function of the device must be obvious.
- The "no knot" method should be simple and straightforward without complex wrapping or weaving, defeating the purpose of going "knot-less".
- The device should solve a real issue or challenge, such as improving dexterity, decreasing/eliminating slippage, improving efficiencies, increasing strength, providing mechanical advantage, minimizing weight, etc.
- The device should pack well. Sharp points, unnecessary bulk, and weight are potential hazards.

If the hardware claims to make things simpler and more manageable, then it should. Unfortunately, some hardware devices are "solutions looking for a problem" or present solutions that are overly complex and maybe not necessary in the first place.

Hardware Pros
- Reduces/eliminates slipping with certain materials.
- Provides quick attachment/detachment.
- Improves adjustability.
- Provides mechanical leverage with reduced friction.

Hardware Cons
- Weight - Gadgets can add significant weight to a system.
- Some hardware gadgets are overly complex and difficult to understand and use.
- Hardware can break, get lost, or be left behind.
- Tends to be expensive.

The best hardware options I've used address specific issues in a simple way. It's like eating salad with a spoon, and then one day someone hands you a fork, and everything changes.

On Knots

Knots and rope work make for an enjoyable pastime that comes with many very practical applications. Unfortunately, as R.M. Abraham said in his 1932 publication "Winter Night's Entertainments".

"It is extraordinary how little the average individual knows about the art of making even the simplest of knots."

I like to break down the thousands of knot variations into two groups: good knots and bad knots. "Good" knots are easily tied, hold fast, and come apart easily when you're done with them. "Bad" knots are all the rest. If you don't believe my definition, perhaps you'll appreciate Lord Robert Baden-Powell's description from the 1908 manual "Scouting for Boys".

"The right kind of knot to tie is one which you can be certain will hold under any amount of strain, and which you can always undo easily if you wish to."

"The bad knot is one which slips away when a hard pull comes on it, or which gets jammed so tight that you cannot untie it."

PRO TIP

Knots are an easy to learn but perishable skill that requires practice.

What Knots Should I Learn?

There are many good knots that have excellent uses for horse riders and campers. The following are the basic workhorse knots that I use regularly.

- Bowline — An excellent all-purpose knot that I often use when setting up a highline. I use the bowline anytime I need a very secure knot.
- Prusik — Made for use in climbing and rappelling, the prusik is a simple knot with a lot of uses, especially when a sliding adjustment is handy. It is especially useful with highlines.
- Trucker's Hitch — A DIY pulley system that is great for tensioning highlines. The 2 to 1 mechanical advantage lets you easily get a highline much tighter than you could by simply pulling on one end.
- Half Hitch – A general use knot that when doubled makes a nice lockdown.

Knot Pros
- Doesn't add weight.
- Versatile (a single knot can be used in multiple applications).
- Knot tying is a skill that (if nurtured), doesn't easily break, get lost, or fail.

Knot Cons
- Knots can reduce the strength of a rope up to 50% (depending on the type of knot used).
- Some knots "bind" when loaded, making them difficult to untie.
- Some ropes are very slippery and don't hold knots well.
- Poorly tied knots can become risks, either to your animal or to yourself.

- If not used often enough, or without practice, you could forget how and when to use knots to their best advantage.

See also Highline, Knots

GLOVES

For trail riders, horse campers, and packers, sturdy gloves go beyond a pleasantry. They are a necessity. Beyond being a comfort when cold or wet, gloves should be required when leading a pack string or working with horses. Rope burn is real and unpleasant, and it can be easily avoided with a pair of gloves.

GOOSENECK - TRAILER

The main difference between a gooseneck trailer and a bumper pull trailer is how it attaches to the tow vehicle. A gooseneck trailer has a long "neck", like that of a goose, that reaches over the back of the tailgate and slides over a ball hitch in the bed of the truck.

The gooseneck hitch is mounted over the truck's rear axle. This centers the trailer's tongue weight over the rear axle of the truck rather than the rear bumper. A benefit of the weight over the truck's axle is that the gooseneck trailer has more stability than a bumper pull. This greater stability allows gooseneck trailers to be longer, wider, and heavier. All these benefits equate to a trailer that can carry more than a bumper pull.

Gooseneck hitches require the installation of special hardware in the bed of the truck. Fortunately, many gooseneck hitches are easily removed for full use of the truck bed when you're not towing.

See also Trailer

GPS

These navigational aids have proven to be lifesavers. However, in the hands of the inexperienced, they can be deadly. More people than ever are venturing into the backcountry without even minimal survival skills. Some riders think of navigation tools as get-out-of-jail-free cards. Many of them will need to be rescued from their incompetence. Before you trust your life to a brick of electronics, learn to use a compass and read a map.

The Global Positioning System, better known simply as GPS, or Global Navigation Satellite System (GNSS), is a tool used to measure distance and help pinpoint locations in any place in the world. GPS does much more than tell you where you are. It is used in everything from heart rate monitors to automobiles.

GPS was first developed and used by the US Department of Defense and allowed for extremely accurate, all-weather navigation for the military. Today, it is used throughout the world in a myriad of devices.

> PRO TIP
> **GPS units are handy, but always carry a traditional map and compass as a backup.**

Surrounding the Earth is a constellation of many manmade satellites. They orbit the globe at different locations about 12,000 miles above the surface of the Earth. They are constantly transmitting information through digital radio signals.

Each of these satellites sends signals to earthbound transmitters at the speed of light. By calculating the length of time it takes for the signal to get to the receiver, the devices are able to make exact measurements. The longer it takes the receiver to receive the signal from the GPS satellite, the farther away the satellite is at that moment. This helps the receiver and the transmitter to deliver precise location information.

The Basic Functions of a GPS Unit

These three functions are common to virtually any GPS receiver suitable for trail riding.

- Location Finding – A GPS unit accurately triangulates your position by receiving data transmissions from multiple orbiting satellites. Your location is given in coordinates, usually latitude and longitude or Universal Transverse Mercator (UTM).
- Navigation – If you have the coordinates for the campsite you're heading to (taken from a map, website, mapping software program, or other sources), a GPS can give you a straight-line, point-to-point bearing, and distance to your destination. Since trails rarely follow a straight line, the GPS' bearing will change as you go. The indicated distance to travel will also decrease as you approach your goal. By combining multiple waypoints on a trail, you can move point-to-point with intermediate bearing and distance guides.

- Tracks – One of the most useful functions of a GPS unit is its ability to lay a virtual "breadcrumb trail" of the route you've taken, called a track. You can configure a GPS to automatically drop "points" at specified intervals of either time or distance. To retrace your steps, simply follow the GPS bearings back through the sequence of track points.

Key Concepts to Remember

A GPS receiver does NOT replace a map and compass or the knowledge of how to use them. Your GPS will supplement and enhance your navigational abilities with technology. You should always carry a detailed map of the area and a compass.

A GPS unit is only as good as the map you use with it. Some of the most useful topographical maps available in the U.S. are the 1:24,000-scale maps published by the U.S. Geological Survey.

Practice! Before using your GPS receiver as a navigational tool in unfamiliar territory, set yourself up for a successful and enjoyable trip by practicing at home in a familiar area. Read the Manual! Familiarize yourself with all the unit's features and controls until you're comfortable with how everything works.

To provide reliable navigational information, a GPS receiver needs to receive good signals from at least three satellites. To see how many satellites your GPS has "acquired", go to the Satellite screen: This will display the current configuration of the satellites and the strength of the signals that are being received.

More satellites are better. If you see only a few satellites and weak signals, your GPS may not provide reliable information.

A clear view of the sky is best for an optimal satellite lock. Tree canopies and canyons can obscure the view overhead and may impede reception.

GPS Navigation Skills to Learn

Reading Coordinates

To simplify map navigation, coordinate systems are used. Coordinates divide the map into a grid and identify a particular location by listing its relative position in terms of north/south and east/west. To choose a coordinate system, find the preferences screen.

The most common coordinate systems used in GPS navigation are:

- DMS (Degrees/Minutes/Seconds): This is the standard way of listing latitude and longitude on paper maps: Example: 48°58'45", -119°56'07".

- DD (Decimal Degree): A decimal version of DMS, made popular by online mapping resources. Example: 48.97929, -119.93517.

- UTM (Universal Transverse Mercator): This military-derived grid system is not tied to latitude and longitude. It divides the map into a square grid with the grid lines 1,000 meters apart. Many topo maps have UTM grid lines printed on them. The system is metric-based and requires no conversion of minutes and seconds. Example: 11U 285238E 5429305N. Here, "11U" identifies the map zone, "285238E" is the east/west or "easting" number, while "5429305N" is the north/south or "northing" number.

Your GPS receiver can automatically display whichever coordinate system you select. Many GPS units also convert coordinates from one system to another. This is helpful if you're given coordinates for a location in one system (e.g., UTM), but want to navigate in another (e.g., DMS).

Entering Waypoints - Plotting a route with waypoints is easy. Simply press the MARK button (Consult the user's manual for your device.). If you're marking a waypoint where you stand, you can often do this with the single press of a button. You can also add multiple levels of detail: a name (e.g., "trailhead" or "camp"), the coordinates, the elevation, and even a short note. This is very helpful if you're marking waypoints for the trail ahead, perhaps before you leave home.

PRO TIP

Before starting a ride, add a waypoint where you've parked your truck and trailer.

Following Waypoints - With waypoints in place, your GPS receiver can guide you from one point to another. Use the FIND or GOTO button to identify a particular waypoint target. Then switch to the compass screen where the GPS receiver will give you a bearing and estimate the distance and time of travel.

Recording Tracks - When you enable the track recording feature, the GPS unit will automatically set track points as you go, essentially laying an electronic breadcrumb trail to show where you've been. With this most useful of tools, your GPS allows you to record time, distance, and path traveled.

You can adjust points to be laid at specified intervals of time or distance. The shorter the distance between track points, the more accurate the path back. The intervals you select should depend on the presence of a marked trail, the terrain, the weather, and other conditions that you find.

Reception Tips

Establishing a good, clear signal is one of the more common complaints from people who have just purchased a GPS receiver. If you experience this, refer to your owner's manual or consider the following:

- Satellite lock: Do this in an open area before you head into the trees where reception is more problematic and variable.
- GPS placement: Fix your receiver to a strap on top of your saddlebags or in your shirt, or coat pocket to give it as clear a view of the sky as possible. If separated from your mount, having the GPS on your person is best.
- Avoid obstacles: A GPS receiver's accuracy (and usefulness) is completely dependent on being able to receive clear transmission signals from three or more satellites. If the "view" to the horizon or overhead is obstructed, that reception could be effectively blocked or diminished, making the GPS unit unreliable. If this occurs, you may need to find an open area. In the meantime, turn off your GPS to conserve battery power.
- Batteries: Make sure they're fresh at the start of your trip. Carry spares.

Stand Alone Versus Dedicated GPS Unit

The question is, does anyone need a standalone GPS anymore? If you own a smartphone, you have a strong case for "no". Countless apps will turn your Android or iPhone into a GPS. Your phone is almost always with you, so it doesn't matter if you're riding on your horse or in your car; you've got GPS.

On the other hand, there are downsides to using your phone as your sole navigation system. For one, there's the matter of power: GPS apps put considerable strain on your smartphone's battery, so if you're riding for more than an hour or two, make sure you have a charger handy. It's a minor hassle, but a hassle all the same.

GRAZING IN THE BACKCOUNTRY

The practicalities of hauling feed make grazing the only reasonable option for backcountry campers. On average, horses need 2% of their body weight per day in feed. If the average horse weighs 1,000 lbs., then it's easy to extrapolate that the animal would require 100 lbs. of feed for a five-day trip. Hauling this in a truck is easy. But when your already overburdened animals, must carry this additional load, along with your camp supplies and equipment, you'll quickly run out of carrying capacity. You'd need another pack animal to haul the extra feed and then another to haul feed for that one. It's a descending spiral of meals for your horses and carrying capacity.

Planning your backcountry adventures around the availability of adequate grazing and water removes the worries of hauling feed. You will have to dedicate time to grazing the critters but watching the ponies grazing peacefully while enjoying your first cup of coffee is one of the best ways to start your day.

See also Feed, Weed Free

GROOMING

A daily go-over for your horses is far more than making your animals look pretty. Whether at home or in camp, each of my animals gets a daily grooming session. These relaxing meetings are much more than just sweeping away sweat and mud. There are many excellent reasons for grooming at home and in camp.

It's a physical exam. Physically touching the animals gives you a lot more information than a cursory glance. Is the horse sensitive in a particular area? Are there any lumps, bumps, or rubs? A good grooming session will let you pick up on these things before they become a trip-ending issue.

Grooming is also a way to say thanks for a great ride.

GROUNDWORK

Smart groundwork with your animals is the foundation for safe and enjoyable trail rides and camping trips. Good ground training helps you establish and reinforce the rules. This helps build trust and confidence in both the horse and the human.

Some of the skills that we work on from the ground include:
- Moving away from pressure.
- Backing up and stepping forward.
- Moving the hind legs.
- Moving the front legs.
- Standing still.

- Focus on the human.
- Desensitization.
- Sending the horse out, over, and around obstacles.
- Moving sideways.
- Dropping the head.
- Lifting and holding a foot up.
- Good leading manners.

NOTE: Mindlessly lunging a horse is not groundwork.

Groundwork also gives you a gauge of a horse's readiness for riding. His reactions to your presence and your cues offer a big hint of how your horse is likely to act when you're in the saddle.
See also Confidence, Training

H

HALF HITCH

The half hitch is a simple knot tied by passing the line's working end around an object, across the main part of the line, and then through the resulting loop. By itself, it's not very useful, but when used in conjunction with other knots, it becomes a valuable component of a wide variety of other hitches. I use single or double half hitches as a "lock" or "stopper" knot that is handy for keeping mischievous horses and mules from untying themselves.

See also Highline, Knots

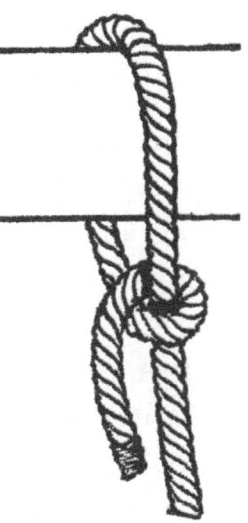

HALTERS

If you've got a horse, you have a halter. It may be plain, fancy, or have special uses, but you've got one laying around. Let's take a peek at some of the different types of halters you find around the barn and spend a little time talking about how and when you will use them.

All halters perform the same function. They provide a tool for controlling horses' movements during handling. But all halters aren't equal. Not every halter is going to suit your needs any more than every halter is going to fit your horse's head perfectly.

The Big Three:

I lump my halter collection into 3 piles. Flat, Round, and Special Purpose. In the following pages we'll check them out.

1 - Flat Halters

As the name implies, flat halters are flat. They are made of strips of flat strapping, connected with metal rings and buckles. I use these forgiving halters when trailering.

Flat Halter Materials

Nylon - Available in a variety of colors and patterns, these halters stand up to the weather and resist abrasion. Nylon halters are very strong, and they're easy to wash and care for. With its wide webbing, a simple nylon halter is my go-to tool for trailering.

Leather - Leather halters look terrific. They offer plenty of strength and durability if they're well taken care of. Well cared for is, of course, the point here. Despite the classic look, feel, and smell of leather, I'd rather be riding than cleaning and oiling tack.

Fitting a Flat Halter

Flat halters come in a variety of sizes such as Cob, Full, and others. Sizing your halter correctly is important for appearance and functionality, ensuring it stays in place properly and is comfortable. To fit your flat halter properly, be sure to use the adjustment points on the crownpiece and noseband. The crownpiece should fit comfortably behind your horse's ears without pinching. The noseband should sit about halfway between your horse's nostrils and eyes. The throatlatch should allow for three to four fingers width so your horse can breathe and swallow properly but won't get a hoof caught. Finally, be sure that the material is not too tight. Properly fitted flat halters evenly distribute pressure and are ideal for trailering.

2 - Round Halters

Round or rope halters are my favorite type of halter for around the barn and on the trail. Rope halters are created from a single piece of rope and forego the prone-to-failure hardware found in flat halters. Because rope halters don't involve any hardware, they are much stronger than flat styles and offer an unfettered connection between handler and horse, allowing for the development of subtle cues.

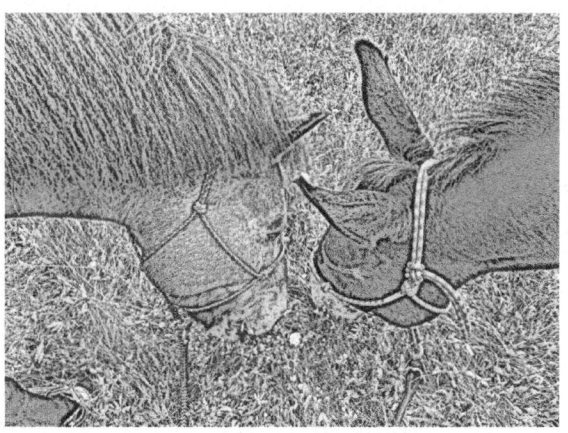

I use rope halters when practicing groundwork at home, under a bridle when trail riding, and when camping with a highline.

How They Work

Rope halters are thinner than leather or nylon halters, so the pressure is more focused versus being distributed across a wider area. As a result, a rope halter will apply a bit of pressure when you want to reinforce a cue.

NOTE: The knots on a rope halter can rub on your horse's face. Watch for this and remove if rub marks begin to happen.

Tying a Rope Halter

Rope halters may not be as instinctual to put on as a flat, but the process will become second nature with a bit of practice. At its heart, a correctly tied rope halter is secured with a sheet bend knot that points back towards the rump.

How to Properly Tie a Rope Halter in 4 Easy Steps:

1) Stand on the near side (left side) of your horse. Reach over the neck and grab the poll strap with your right hand.
2) Slide the noseband over the horse's nose and the throat knot upwards below the jaw.
3) Take the end of the poll strap pointing towards you and run it through the tie loop.
4) Run the end of the poll strap behind the loop and then tuck through the space between the loop and the strap. For the more

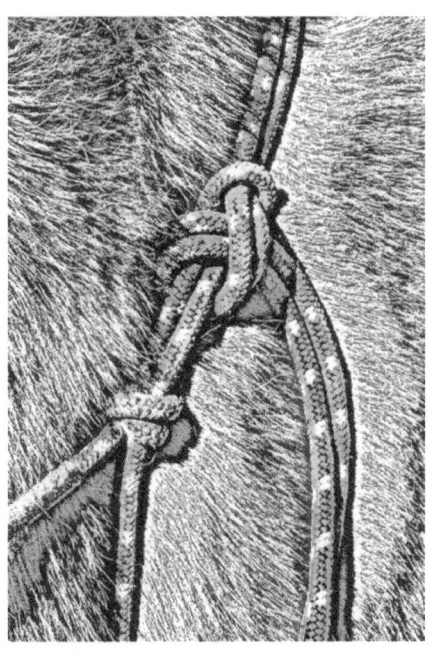

technically inclined what you just did was create a sheet bend knot!
   a. Make sure that the pointy end is pointing towards your animal's butt and away from his eye!

3 - Special Purpose Halters

There are many types of special purpose halters available from grooming to shipping. The two most common special purpose halters that I see are leading / packing halters and breakaway halters.

Leading/Packing – Also known as side pull halters, these tools help keep the animal you're ponying from pulling back on you while going down the trail. The halter tightens as they pull back, and the animal quickly learns that the easiest way down the trail is without pulling. These can be found with chain or leather pulls. I like my "come along nicely" halters to  have a wide leather nose piece, so they're a bit more comfortable.

Breakaway Halters – These flat-style halters typically have a breakable crown piece that acts as a fuse in case something exciting happens. My preference is, I don't want my equipment to break. If a horse tied with a breakaway halter gets free, you have trained him to walk away whenever he wants. That could be a very bad thing. For me, the risks from running free outweigh those of staying put. Lost horses in the wilderness rarely come to good ends, and even in a front country camp, a free-roaming equine could cause injury to others. I choose to avoid breakaways; you'll have to decide what works best for you.

Of course, I spend a significant amount of time with my animals, and they have earned the privilege of being tied. Until I can reliably saddle and unsaddle without the aid of tying, my animals aren't ready for the trail or the opportunity to rest and relax while parked to a trailer, tree, or highline.

I also hear from people who say they keep halters on their animals so they can catch them. To that, I say that both the human and the beast need more training. Teach your critters to come when called.

HAMMOCK

When riding the backcountry across remote mountain ridges and miles of seemingly untouched terrain, being comfortable is one of your top priorities. A good night's sleep makes the difference between a beautiful day on the trail or a rough and miserable day spent battling back pain.

With the wide variety of options available for backcountry shelters, it's important to know what best fits your needs before going online and ordering the cheapest option.

I spend a fair amount of the summer on the trail and in the backcountry, so when I first talked with a Pacific Crest Trail through-hiker about hammocks for camping, I was intrigued. At that point, for me, a hammock was a wonderful backyard nap instrument, and that was it. I didn't realize that in the past few years, hammock technology has made huge steps forward and can provide a versatile and economical shelter suitable for a wide variety of situations. The unique features that hammocks offer are also helpful when it comes to comfort and pack-ability. These many benefits make hammocks a good option for packing into a backcountry camp. Let's take a more in-depth look into their advantages.

Hammocks are viable options anywhere there's an elevated attachment point. For most of us, that means trees. You can quickly see how a hammock isn't limited to that magic unicorn of a campsite where the ground is clear, level, free of rocks, roots, and spiders. This versatility opens many wonderful camping areas that previously weren't accessible.

Most hammocks are much lighter than the average tent and, with no rigid poles, are able to be stuffed into a very small area. This makes them ideal for riders camping off of their riding animals as well as packers wanting to save some space. An additional point worth mentioning is how quick a hammock can go from pack to "home sweet home". The setup time for a hammock is usually much less than that of setting up a tent. When the weather's fine, this isn't a big deal. When it's cold, and the rain clouds are rushing in, it's a wonderful thing.

Apart from the lightweight, small volume, and ease of setup, it's the comfort factor of hammocks that keeps me elevated. With no hard rocks digging into your back, no slope that oozes you downhill during the night, and no worries about wet ground seeping in, a good night's sleep is assured. As long as you've got a couple of trees nearby, you can choose to slumber anywhere that you like.

The Learning Curve - The first few times that you use your hammock, it will take a bit of getting used to. You'll find that there is a bit of a knack for a comfortable night's sleep. Let's discuss some of the fine points of hammocking.

- Cold Butt Syndrome – Just as when you're sleeping on the ground, the insulation of your sleeping bag will be compressed beneath you. Compressed insulation equals no insulation. To combat this, there are a variety of solutions, from custom-made under quilts that hang beneath the hammock to a low-cost closed-cell foam pad that you lay on inside the hammock.

- The Squeeze – First-time hammock users tend to stretch their hammock too tightly in an effort to make the hammock straight. It generally doesn't work. Instead, hang your hammock with a deep sag. It's this sag that allows you to lay flat and even sleep on your side.

- The Fall – "I'd fall out" is often the first thing I hear from the uninitiated. The solution is to set up your hammock with a deep sag. Do this, and it's almost impossible to have an unplanned exit.

- Singles Only – One of the downfalls of hammocking is that, at this point, it's very difficult for couples to snooze together without some discomfort.

As you see, hammocks, like most things, do have some downfalls. Squeezing two people into a hammock can be daunting, and it'll be cramped. Staying warm can be a challenge. My first hanging experience was "memorable". I had packed high into the Norse Peak Wilderness in Washington's Cascade Range. What I didn't think about was the amount of convective heat loss from the air under and around the hammock. It was a rude introduction to the reality of Cold Butt Syndrome, and I spent the longest part of the night huddled by the campfire; not fun. I've since refined the system and thankfully haven't repeated those particular mistakes.

My Setup – Of the four hammocks I have, I most often use a cheap department store model. It weighs the least, packs smaller, and costs less than any of the others. It also comes with a built-in mosquito net that helps to ensure a good nights' rest.  With the addition of a small tarp, this setup offers a rainproof, mosquito-proof shelter plus a covered line to dry and protect any camping gear or tack.

Despite some temperature and space restrictions, I've found hammocks are an excellent alternative to the classic tent approach. Hammocks can provide a comfortable and versatile solution for anyone from the weekend rider to packers venturing into the backcountry for weeks at a time.

HEAT

Summer: It's a time to enjoy the long days with long rides as you enjoy the sultry warmth of the season. Before you hit the trails, spend a quick minute thinking about the very real risks of riding in the heat. Heat Stress, Exhaustion, and Stroke, along with the complications from them, are risks that, if not recognized and treated correctly, can be debilitating and even life-threatening for your horse.

The hallmark of summer is heat and humidity. The Effective

Temperature or Heat Stress Index test is a quick and easy tool to help determine when environmental conditions may be likely to result in heat-related illness. This test consists of simply adding together the ambient temperature and the relative humidity. Veterinary professionals recommend that riders use caution when the sum of the ambient temperature in degrees Fahrenheit and the relative humidity is around 150. When those figures approach 180, most riding activities involving long or intense exercise should be postponed, so heat build-up doesn't become critical.

Many horse owners don't realize that only about 25% of the energy used in a horse's working muscles is converted to actual muscle movement. The remaining 75% loss of efficiency is represented by waste heat that becomes very difficult for the horse to disperse in hot and humid weather.

A conditioning program will help your mount become more efficient at dissipating this waste heat. Horses and humans get rid of excess heat in large part by sweating. An out of shape horse's sweat can be a foamy lather that contains high concentrations of vital electrolytes that does not evaporate quickly. Obese horses are further hampered by a thick fat layer that traps heat inside.

As a horse becomes fitter, less demand is placed on the working muscles, and ultimately, he becomes much more efficient at dissipating heat. Less exertion (better condition) means less heat generated by the muscles; less heat means less sweat, less sweat means less fluid and electrolyte loss. As the horse's body conserves and utilizes electrolytes and minerals, less of these body salts are lost through sweating. This, in turn, alters the consistency of the sweat itself, making it thinner and more easily evaporated, thus more effectively cooling the skin.

Common sense, a sensible conditioning schedule, and the ability to recognize the warning signs of heat stress will help your horse, and yourself safely weather the warm summer months.

PRO TIP

Keeping your horse in shape through the winter and spring will help him adjust more easily to summer's higher temperatures and increased physical demands.

Heat exhaustion and stroke refer to dangerous conditions that are most likely to occur when horses work hard in the heat, especially if they are working beyond their fitness level. While often used interchangeably, they should be more precisely defined. Heat exhaustion is a situation when the horse is dehydrated and exhausted from overheating. A horse suffering from heat exhaustion will be tired and very hot but should revive with treatment (rest, water, and cooling). Heatstroke is a total collapse and more life-threatening. A horse in heatstroke is in imminent danger of dying.

One of the main ways a horse cools himself is by sweating and utilizing the evaporation of sweat to dissipate body heat. However, in hot, humid conditions, the air is already damp, and sweat won't evaporate. The horse stays hot, and the body keeps signaling for more sweating; the horse stays wet with sweat but doesn't get any cooler. If the horse runs out of fluid due to excessive sweating, dehydration has occurred. A dehydrated horse is always at risk because he can no longer cool himself by sweating, and his temperature will continue to rise.

Signs of dehydration include:
- Mouth and gums that are dry, brick red, or very pale. (Mucous membranes should be a healthy pink color. Now pry yourself away from this book and go check your horse's gums.)
- Loss of skin elasticity – A pinch of skin pulled out from the neck or shoulder that does not spring right back into place, but instead, stays tented for several seconds is a sign of dehydration. If it takes 2 or 3 seconds for the skin to sink back into place, the horse is moderately dehydrated, if it stays elevated for 6 to 10 seconds or longer, he is severely dehydrated.
- Poor capillary refill time – Press your finger into his gum and remove. If the spot stays white and pale for a few seconds meaning the blood doesn't rush right back afterward, the horse is dehydrated.
- Heart rate also increases as the horse's body tries to get more blood to the surface for cooling but has less body fluid to do it with.
- Loss of fluid will also make the horse's eyes seem to sink back into his head and his eyelids and tissues around the eyes appear wrinkled.

Horses and mules exhibiting these symptoms should be rested, watered, and cooled. If the condition doesn't right itself, it's time to contact your veterinarian.
See also Vital Signs

HELLO – JUST SAY IT
There's an expression in French: Simple comme bonjour, "simple as hello". No matter what language you use, French, Japanese, German,

or others, it's as simple as "hello".

Do you greet the folks you're sharing the trail with? You should. A friendly *"Howdy"* when you meet someone on the trail will help horse riders become everyone's favorite trail partners. A hello can also help keep you safe. The hiker you politely greeted could be the vital link that directs Search and Rescue to your location after a wreck that leaves you hurt and scared along the trail. You want the people  you encounter on the trail to remember meeting you. Hello is a great way to start a conversation. Ask about the trail conditions ahead, water sources, or how far until the next trail junction or campsite.

Being polite, offering a friendly *"Shalom,"* and encouraging the people we share the trails with to engage in a brief chat will also help your horse to understand that the strange lycra-clad beast ahead is indeed just another odd human and not an equine eating creature to fear.

An *"Aloha"* when coming across other trail users will help break the stereotype of horsemen as rude, inconsiderate, and even dangerous. If we want to pause the cycle of trail loss, horse riders need to be perceived in a more positive light. We're able to do that in a variety of different ways, starting with saying hello and being polite.

Have you ever been riding when someone greeted you with a *"Hello"*, and it made you feel good? We all have. Those experiences underscore the power of a simple greeting. When you say hello to someone, you're acknowledging them, and we all love to be acknowledged. Every time we fail to say hello when we pass another trail user is a lost opportunity to make a positive difference in the world.

I'm energized when a simple hello turns into a positive interaction. The opposite is true of the less-than-stellar times when "*Guten tag*" falls on deaf ears. We feed off of one another's energy, which is why we feel so wonderful at the end of a good ride but leave the DMV feeling like a drink is in order. When a sincere trail greeting is ignored, it's easy for us to feel awkward, silly, and even mad. Mother Teresa once said, "Every time you smile at someone, it is an action of love, a gift to that person, a beautiful thing". When I think of greetings as a gift, it is easier to be OK with receiving nothing in return. I like to give gifts just because I can, without any expectation of reciprocation.

You don't have to say "*Konnichiwa*" to everyone. Although I try to make it a point to say hello to all I meet on the trail, an exception is the rare event when you happen upon someone who makes you feel unsafe. Keep moving in those situations, pull out a cell phone if you have one, or pretend that you're with a group that is just behind you.

The vast majority of our trail encounters are pleasant experiences that could be made even better if we take the time to say "*Hola*" and mean it. Don't underestimate the power a hello can have on your fellow trail users. A hello costs you nothing yet brightens the spirits of others and yourself. That's powerful.

If we say *"Bonjour"* just half the time we pass someone on the trail, we'll be making a huge difference and improving the world.
See also Etiquette

HELMET

Long-time riders, as well as novices, have accidents. Horse riding is statistically more dangerous than downhill skiing and motorcycling. Avoid becoming a statistic by wearing a quality riding helmet. Every ride. Every time.

Horseback riding has been identified as a higher-risk activity than automobile racing, motorcycle riding, football, and skiing. Injuries occur while riding or handling horses without discrimination for age or experience level. Approximately 70,000 people are treated in emergency rooms annually because of equestrian-related injuries, while thousands more receive treatment in physicians' offices. Head injuries account for about 60% of deaths resulting from equestrian accidents.

Wearing a helmet can significantly reduce the chances of sustaining serious injury. One of the most important pieces of safety equipment is a properly fitting helmet. These tools absorb impacts to the head, provide a cushion for the skull and reduce the jarring of the brain against the skull. The New England Journal of Medicine has reported that wearing helmets reduces head and brain injuries by 85%. The

Equestrian Medical Safety Association strongly recommends wearing a properly fitted ASTM/SEI certified equestrian helmet with the harness secured during equestrian activities.

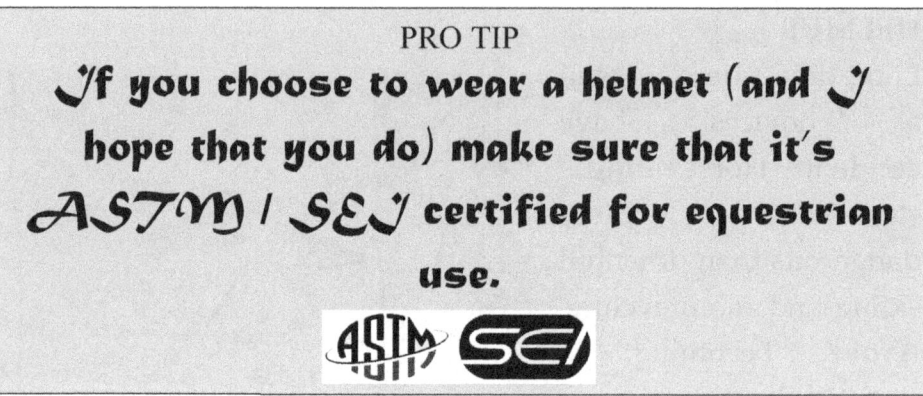

PRO TIP

If you choose to wear a helmet (and I hope that you do) make sure that it's ASTM / SEI certified for equestrian use.

How does a riding helmet protect your head? Riding helmets reduce the risk of severe head and brain injury by limiting the force of a shock to the head. They do this by acting as a barrier between the skull and whatever's causing the impact. The helmet absorbs the energy of the impact and reduces the force that the skull and brain feel. It disperses the force of the impact over a wider area, preventing the energy from concentrating in one spot. At the same time as absorbing the impact, riding helmets also have a hard outer shell designed to reduce the risk of penetration by sharp objects. This outer shell covers an expanded polystyrene lining that absorbs and disperses the impact. To work correctly, your helmet must fit properly and have a properly fastened chin strap.

Do riding helmets work? If you're not sure whether wearing a helmet is a good idea or not, you might want to consider that the most frequent cause of death or serious injury amongst horse activities (both mounted and dismounted) are head injuries. That's a scary thought. When you consider that most deaths from a head injury could be prevented by wearing a riding helmet, it's shocking that only 20% of riders wear one.

How do I choose a riding helmet? To determine the right helmet, you must measure your head. To  measure your head, use a soft measuring tape around the widest part of your head (approximately an inch above your eyebrows); this will give you a measurement that you can compare against the manufacturer's size chart. Each manufacturer will have a unique size chart, and there will be some variations between them.

Once you know what size helmet you need, you should then begin to try them on, a correctly fixed helmet should sit snugly, cover your entire skull, and have even pressure all around. There shouldn't be any gaps, the helmet shouldn't ride up or slide down, and the helmet's brim should be around two fingers distance above the eyebrows.

HIGHLINE
If you're an experienced horse camper or want to be an experienced horse camper, you've most likely either used or have heard of the "high" "line". When done well, a highline is an exceptionally useful low-impact method for keeping our furry four-legged friends out of mischief. When done poorly, few things give the equestrian community a worse reputation.

In the next few pages you'll find more information on these remarkable tools.

Just as cooking a great campfire meal requires following a few simple steps, setting up a safe and effective highline requires a few easy steps and only three main ingredients that you most likely already have.

Highline Ingredient List

1)   **2 Stout Objects** – At its simplest, a highline is just a rope tied between two stable objects such as trees or even horse trailers. Since horse trailers and pre-built facilities are lacking in most backcountry scenarios, look for live, sturdy trees at least 8 to 10 inches in diameter. Look up and check for dead branches that could fall. Failure to select the right supports for your highline will be a self-correcting problem that you won't soon repeat.

2)   **1 Pair Tree Saver Straps** – As their name implies, these 2 to 3-inch-wide webbing straps protect trees by minimizing girdling and damage to the bark and cambium layer of trees. Tree savers are the law in many areas and are highly encouraged everywhere else. Using

tree savers helps to ensure that equestrian use will continue to be permitted for years to come. Many styles are available. Some have rings built-in, and some even include adjustable buckles. I prefer tree savers that are brightly colored so that they are less apt to be misplaced

and forgotten. Discarded cinches or car seat belts are good alternatives for the penny pinchers among us.

3)   **Rope** – This is the component your animals will be tied to, so you want a material that won't break or stretch when pulled on by several 1,000+ pound animals. "Skookum" (from the Salish word for big – strong – mighty) is a good thing to look for in a highline rope. Make sure that it's Skookum strong.

How long should a highline rope be? I'm a believer in "more is better". It's better to have rope not used than wishing for "just a few more feet". I generally carry 50 to 100-foot lengths. My favorite highline rope material is polypropylene because it has less stretch than nylon, doesn't absorb water, and feels good in the hand. A 3/8 inch, three-strand polyester rope is plenty strong (over 2,400 pounds breaking strength) and more resistant to abrasion than other materials. Pretty much any

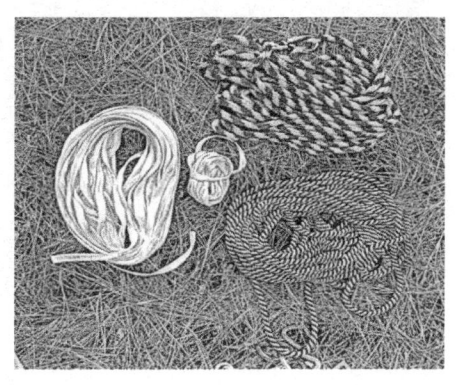

modern good-quality rope, properly treated against UV damage, is extraordinarily resilient and will last for many years.

Highline Ingredient Variations:

- Carabiners – These lightweight, metal snap-links are used in a wide variety of tasks. While not a necessity, including a few carabiners into your highline recipe adds versatility by providing quick attachment points, improved adjustability, reduced friction, and increased mechanical advantage (leverage for tightening). If you choose to use carabiners, be sure to use devices certified for rock climbing, NOT the cheap links sold at the checkout line.
- Swivels – Keeps lead lines from twisting. Devices certified for rock climbing are stronger than those found at most tack stores.
- Knot eliminators and rope winches – For knot-averse campers. These gadgets tend to be expensive, heavy, and often redundant "solutions" that sometimes create more unwanted hassles. Use them at your peril.

Highline Assembly

"Mise en Place" is a French term that translates into "putting in place" and is used in professional kitchens when organizing ingredients for a meal. As horse campers, we can use this practice to make our camping experience more efficient by helping prevent mistakes or forgetting crucial ingredients when you need them most.

1) Find a Good Location – Where we set up our highline is very important.
   a) Don't keep stock too close to camp. Placing your highline away from your immediate campsite will help you get a better night's sleep as well as keep your campsite much cleaner for you and future campers. Camping amongst manure piles isn't pleasant.
   b) Pick a location where the damage from trampling hooves will be minimized, such as hard-packed dirt or rocky soils.
   c) Your highline should be at least 100 feet away from water sources such as streams or lakes (some areas require a longer distance).
2) Place the Tree Savers – Wrap your tree saver straps around the two trees you've selected. Place the tree savers as high as possible, so the highline is above the horse's head. I try to set them at least seven feet high.
3) Lay Out the Highline Rope – Loosely stretch your rope between the tree savers and tie one end to the first tree saver strap with a quick-release Bowline knot.
4) Tie an inline loop in the rope 7-8 feet from the second tree
   a) The Alpine butterfly is secure and very easy to untie when breaking camp. An alternative is a Prusik loop.
5) Run the remaining rope through the second tree saver and back through the inline loop that you made in step #4.

a) With this arrangement, you've just created what is known as a "Trucker's Hitch," a type of block and tackle arrangement that gives you a 2-to-1 mechanical advantage and the ability to get the rope good and tight.

6) Pull tight and secure with a couple of Half-Hitches. Tuck any left-over rope behind the tree where a curious horse cannot get to it.

7) Decide where to place ties for your horses' lead lines and attach a prusik loop at each point. I add a swivel to each prusik.
a) Make sure to place tie points so that the horses cannot chew or rub on the trees or get into mischief with one another.

8) Tie horses lead ropes into the Prusik loops with a quick-release knot. Attach a carabiner to the Prusik and then tie leads to that to eliminate twisting as the horse turns.

Now that we've demystified the recipe for a highline, you're ready for years of safe and enjoyable horse camping!
See also Alpine Butterfly, Bowline, Containment, Half-Hitch, Knots, Prusik, Trucker's Hitch, Online Resources

HOBBLES

If you frequently venture into the backcountry and beyond the

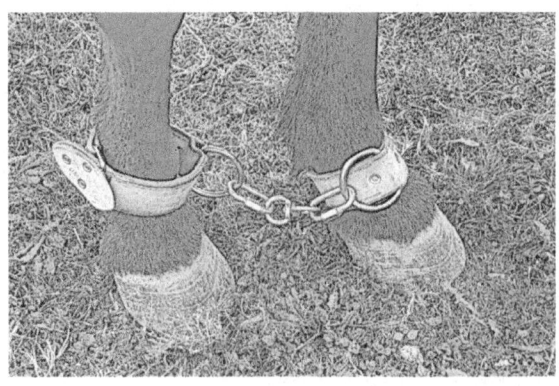

reassuring safety of the trailhead, you probably already have a working knowledge of hobbles. Unfortunately, many horse owners have never seen or used these remarkable and versatile tools. Even if we don't regularly venture into the wilderness, hobbles can play a useful role. Indeed, hobbles are an excellent aid for every rider.

First, let's briefly discuss what hobbles are. Simply put, hobbles are devices that limit the locomotion of stock by securing two or more legs. Like a pair of handcuffs, when placed around the pastern or cannon bones, hobbles will limit the range of movement of your animal. This will help to keep him somewhat near where you left him.

On trail rides, I'll often take hobbles to let my horse graze during lunch instead of tying him up. If I'm eating and taking a break, why not let him grab a bite as well?

Hobbles also make backcountry camping without packing in feed much more doable. With a set of hobbles and good grazing, your horse is able to forage for his breakfast, lunch, and dinner saving you a lot of weight and room in your saddlebags.

Just as horses come in a range of shapes and sizes, hobbles are also available in various types and materials. Figure eights, chain, sideline, Mormon, and hard bar are just a few variations of the common two-leg hobble, and each has its strengths and weaknesses depending upon your intended use. I'm partial to a buckle-less version which eliminates any awkward fumbling with straps and fasteners on cold, wet mountain mornings. Two other popular types of

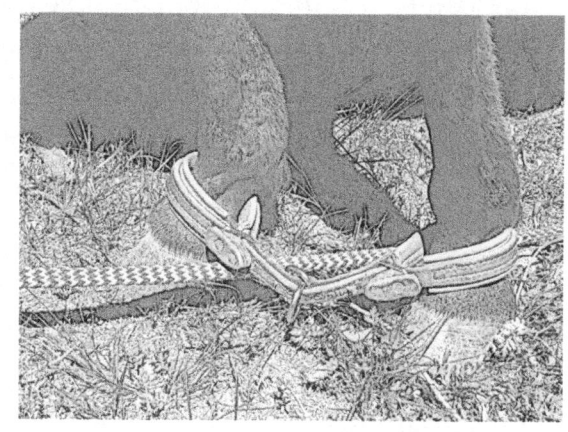

hobbles are the "Figure Eight" and "Two Ring" (also known as a Utah) hobble. A benefit of both of these types of hobbles is the ability to strap them around your mount's neck, making them very easy to get to when it's time to take a break while riding.

When looking for a set of hobbles, look for robust construction and heavy-duty materials. Hobbles are one area that I forego my usual mantra of lightweight materials. Early in my explorations of hobbles, I tried a nylon set, and despite having heavy felt padding, my mount paid the price with nasty rub burns on his pasterns from the tendency of felt to collect and hold dirt. After that experience, I've changed to smooth leather hobbles that don't collect debris and are easy to clean.

When I use hobbles, I always give the area where I'm turning the animals out a quick look over to ensure that there aren't any hazards present before I release the beasts. Obstacles such as holes, fallen trees, boulders, and such can be too much for an animal to navigate when hobbles hinder their movement. I like to think of hobbles as devices for areas where I have verified the footing and safety first.

In addition to helping to slow a horse on his way back to the trailer while you're still in your tent, hobbles are wonderful Leave No Trace (LNT) tools. Stock with a pawing habit can make a big mess while they're on a highline. Hobbles will stop that in short order. I've also used hobbles to keep horses from pawing at the trailhead while we're tacking up for a ride.

HOBBLE TRAINING
For your safety and that of your stock, train your horses to be comfortable in hobbles. This is valuable at home and especially important for backcountry travel.

Training horses to accept hobbles begins with teaching them to respect ropes around their legs. I want the animals to give to pressure on their legs. Practice leading your horse with a rope looped around a leg.

Using a thick, soft, rope catch a front leg starting behind the knee and moving down to the horse's pastern. The leg should not be tied or trapped. If the horse gets scared, simply let go of one end of the rope to release the animal.

With the leg caught, ask the horse to take a step by applying pressure to the rope and pulling the leg forward. When it begins to move forward, release the pressure. Do this exercise with all four legs until you are able to lead the horse anywhere you want to go. At this point, you're ready for the hobbles.

When getting my animals familiar with hobbles, I introduce them during a late dinner. In a large area with safe footing, I give them a flake of choice hay. They're more interested in eating than the hobbles I'm putting on their front legs. Tug on the hobbles, so the horse knows he is being restrained. Horses and mules are generally more absorbed in filling their stomachs than fighting the hobbles. Repeat this process often, and soon your animals will come to regard hobbles as a welcome precursor to dinner. Don't leave hobbled horses unattended.

A benefit of hobble training is that if the horse gets a leg stuck in a fence or wire, he'll be less likely to panic and better prepared to stand still and wait for help.

HUNTING SEASON RIDING TIPS

Autumn's crisp temperatures, golden foliage, and glorious weather beckon both hunters and horse riders alike to enjoy the season in the outdoors.

Don't miss the pleasure of a fall ride when the air is crisp, the bugs are gone, the crowds are scarce, and — with the leaves off the trees — the views are terrific. The following five "Be"s will help ensure a safe hunting season ride.

Be Knowledgeable – Before you load the horse in the trailer, familiarize yourself with where and when hunting is taking place so that you can plan your ride accordingly. A quick internet search of your state's Natural Resources, or Fish and Game,

Department's website will arm you with information on what game is in season and dates when hunters will be out in force. Knowing the season's dates will give you valuable ammunition in planning a ride. Where I grew up, the deer season is short and fierce. Simply doing arena work and skipping the trails on opening day was sufficient. In other areas hunting seasons run from late August and past Thanksgiving, and that's entirely too long to stay off the trails. During this time of year, I try to ride in more open areas where hunters can see me more easily. It's also a good time to stick to well-traveled trails and avoid cross-country travel through brushy areas.

Be Prepared – Is your animal ready for the sounds and sights of hunting season? For the unprepared, the first notice of hunting season is the loud report of gunfire. We've all heard, and some have experienced, the old story of the dude asking if he can shoot from horseback and the reply was yes... Once. Although I'm sure they exist, I don't know any horse, or mule for that matter, which is 100% ok with gunfire. Heck, I get antsy when I hear it. That being said, I'm happy as long as my animals tolerate the sounds of shooting. Getting to that point takes time and patience but is doable. Many riders start this training with a cap gun and slowly work their way up to louder devices. Find your local mounted shooting club for help in how to do it.

Hunting season brings not only loud noises but also new encounters on the trails. After we've trained hard all summer getting our mounts used to bicycles and hikers, we now need to be concerned about meeting trains of pack mules heading into and out of hunt camps. In addition to the pack trains, we'll also want to be prepared for when the earth rises when a camouflaged hunter stands up as we ride by. I'll never forget the rodeo that happened the time a tree waved, and a very well camouflaged turkey hunter said hello. I'm not sure who was more startled, my horse or me.

Be Bright – Game animals largely come in shades of brown or black. You certainly don't want to be confused for a deer or other prey so make sure to stand out with bright-colored clothing for you and your mount. Blaze orange is a long-time standby and is required for hunters to wear in many states. With a brightly colored jacket or vest, you'll stand out from the background and be easily recognized. What's good for the rider is also good for the horse. There are many suppliers of brightly colored tack, and riding equipment that is made just for horses. This gear looks like nothing generally found in nature and will keep your trail buddy from being mistaken for a deer or elk. When I lived in a more rural area where hunting occurred near my property, I kept blaze orange on my animals even in their pasture and paddock areas. Better safe than sorry.

Be a Little Noisy – I become a bigger fan of bells during the hunting season. Just as I use bells to prevent a surprise meeting with an ursine family during spring and summer, I keep them on during hunting season lest I accidentally fall prey to something other than the local bear population. Between the bright colors and the soft jingle of the bell attached to my cinch, everyone in my immediate vicinity knows that I'm nearby. One point to consider is that while we want to remain as safe as possible, we don't want to interfere with the hunt; in fact, to do so is illegal. Creating excessive noise isn't going to make you any safer and could give a wrong impression of the equine community at large.

Be Friendly – Should you come across a hunter on your ride, you may want to give them a quiet "thank you" for their contribution in keeping your access to trails open. The primary drivers in creating the National Forests, Wilderness areas, and many public lands were the naturalists and hunters of the early 1900s. So, although hunting may not be your sport of choice, the contributions of hunters significantly add to the preservation of wild areas that all can enjoy.

There you go. Riders needn't fear the fall woods. Horse riders and hunters alike share a love of the outdoors and should be working together to understand our shared values. Outdoor people of all types are on the same side regarding the responsible use of public lands.

ABCs of Horse Camping

I

INJURY

Despite our best planning, accidents will happen. Being prepared can often prevent and help you treat typical trail riding and horse camping woes.

The most common issues that we see are cuts, scrapes, and abrasions caused by ill-fitting tack and trail hazards. The vast majority of these are annoying but not serious. Before you head out, talk with your veterinarian and your physician about how to treat these nearly inevitable dings to both your animals and you.

You'll want to have the knowledge and equipment to immediately address the situation for the rare but more severe injuries that you may encounter. Find and take courses on 1st Aid, build a proper emergency kit and have the knowledge to use it.

See also Emergency Plan, Essentials, First Aid

A Memorable Ride

Outside an emergency room entrance, a strange town stretching ahead. Wobbling. Unsteady on new crutches, a hospital issue suit of sweatpants and t-shirt, a single anti-slip sock completed the ensemble. A flimsy plastic bag held all my belongings; a vial of narcotics and $150 in cash. I had no wallet, ID, or phone; it was not a good way to end a day.

The Continental Divide Trail ranged ahead towards its terminus in Canada. Closer was the famed Chinese Wall in Montana's Bob Marshall Wilderness Complex. Closer yet was our lunch destination in the aptly named Pretty Prairie.

The South Fork of the Sun River sparkled before us as it raced to the Gulf of Mexico over 1,000 miles away via the Missouri and Mississippi Rivers. We would cross the Sun twice before making it to our luncheon spot near the Pretty Prairie patrol cabin overlooking a clearing in the forest.

Preparing for a pack trip is an involved process that becomes more so the longer the trip and the more people coming along. The basics of food, water, and shelter are the same for any camping trip. Complications grow with the number of people and animals accompanying you and the number of days you'll be out. Our group of 4 humans and eight mules and horses were heading out on a ten-day 85-mile pack trip. This was the first trip into the

ABCs of Horse Camping

Bob for my three companions, and I wanted it to be special. As it turned out, it was quite memorable for all involved.

This early-season trip was one of my few recreational runs into the 1.5-million-acre expanse of the Bob Marshall. Most of my previous visits to this spectacular country had involved hauling tools and materials for backcountry work parties, not the lounging and loafing that I was looking forward to on this adventure.

Below me, reaching up to Ruger's knees, the river rushed over the polished green, gray, red, and black stones. Each rock told a story of time and geology before forming the shifting and slippery riverbed below Ruger's shoes. Having passed through this ford many times over the years, I knew that if the river were knee-deep 10 feet from the bank, it would be belly-deep by midstream. That would mean my short statured pack animals might have to swim if we continued. Caution being the better part of valor, I decided that this side of the Sun would make for a fine, much drier lunch spot with acres of ample grazing for the mules. With the pack string in tow, we turned into the current, facing upstream to exit the river and make our way on to lunch.

It may be cliché, but time moved slowly as Ruger first shifted his weight and attempted to navigate the unstable stones under the surface. He then dropped onto his side, my leg trapped under his bulk as I sat on the riverbed, water up to my chest. Once the current caught his mass, the big red mule rolled over me, forcing me underwater as we spun over one another on our way downstream. My much better half Celeste had a ringside seat for the show as Ruger and I tumbled in the swift river. Things had become sporty.

By the time I lunged and heaved out of the river like a half-drowned rat, Celeste was already at the bank and helped reunite me with dry land. Other than coughing up quite a bit of the frigid river water, I thought all was well *if a bit wet. Then I tried to stand up. Ruger fared much better than I. He clambered ashore wet but otherwise unharmed save for a few bumps and scrapes.*

Thank Heavens for trained medical personnel. One of our companions was a nurse and immediately went to work assessing what impacts my unplanned mule rafting journey had wrought. Celeste and I both keep current with our 1st Aid and CPR certifications but having a professional on hand made things a lot less frightening.

It was quickly determined that riding out was not going to be the best option. It was time to call for help.

Satellite messengers are game-changers, and we don't go off-grid without one. Most of the time, they're simply a reliable tool for communicating with family and friends when cell coverage is a dream. It's during exciting times that the utility of these handheld devices comes home. For the past several years, I've carried satellite messenger devices that use a cell phone as the interface and display. These SM units have always handled all my needs. Until the phone broke.

The downfall of keeping the 10 essentials on your person is that if you have a wreck, there's a chance that your emergency tools can be damaged. Despite a strong protective case, water pouring from the insides of the battered phone told a tale of irreparable damage. The SM wasn't coming to the rescue today.

The space shuttle had redundant systems, and so should you. We always carry backups for critical systems, including communications. Celeste carries a Personal Locator Beacon from ACR on our rides. A PLB may not be able to send non-emergency messages, but it also has no subscription fees. We've carried the PLB for years without having to utilize it. Now was the time to put our "when the stuff hits the fan" tool to use.

Once the PLB was activated, the only thing left was to wait for the signal to make its way from space to a US Air Force command center in Florida, then on to the Helena, MT Sheriff's Office, where they arranged aviation support from Two Bear Air. Once the helicopter rotors were 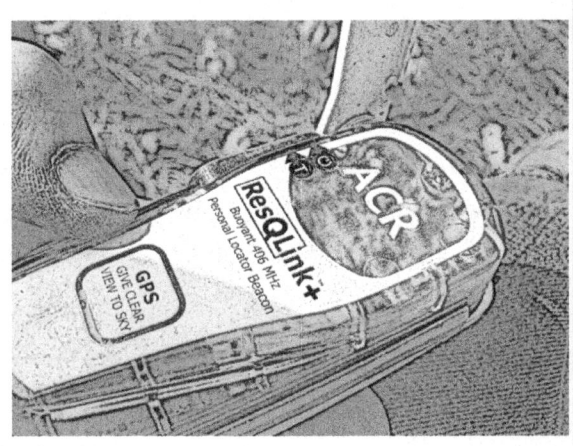 spinning, it was a 52-minute flight from Kalispell, MT to my location at the confluence of the south and west forks of the Sun River. In only three hours, word of my wreck had traveled thousands of miles and coast to coast and back and returned to my riverbank in the form of two paramedics and a pilot traveling in a shiny blue helicopter. A PLB works.

Snacks are always welcome. Especially in an emergency. Not only did the gleaming Bell helicopter arrive with two paramedics ready to work on their patient, but the pilot also brought freshly baked banana bread that he shared with my companions as the paramedics readied me for transport.

The twin engines of a Bell GlobalRanger create over 1,100 horsepower, and the pilot whipped each horse as he sped to Helena 80 air miles and many mountain ridges away. My journey from a dusty riverbank to a spotless ER took only 34 minutes. Celeste's trip out of the Bob was going to take much longer as she singlehandedly led the pack string of 3 mules and a horse back to the trailhead miles away.

ER staff determined that I had neatly relocated part of my lower leg bone, specifically the medial malleolus. For the layman, this is the projection on the inside of your ankle. Find it, then imagine the bump moved to a brand-new location. Injuries like these hurt like heck, but they're a long way from the heart. Once the Docs and Nurses had me stabilized and ready for an orthopedic surgeon to take over, it was time to turn me loose on the town of Helena.

This is where the day continued its interesting turns. My wallet, with ID, credit cards, and cash, jumped ship at some point during my river excursion. Although the ER staff had arranged overnight accommodations, my lack of ID proved troublesome as I tried to check into the hotel. After more trouble than it should have been and multiple phone calls back to the hospital, they reluctantly agreed to accept my hospital wristband as ID and let me into a room. It would be a long night waiting for transportation the following morning to get me home and into a surgery theatre over 8 hours away.

That my friends, is the story of a memorable pack trip into the Bob. After every ride, my wife and I go through a post-trip debrief to see where things could have been better and how we can improve our future trips. There's been a lot of discussion regarding this adventure. I don't know what we could have done differently. We didn't take untoward risks. Indeed, the accident happened as I was avoiding a potentially dangerous situation. We were prepared and equipped for emergencies, and our system redundancy plans worked well. Sometimes accidents happen, and I feel that this was one of those times.

INSECTS

Some will tell aspiring trail riders to fear the bears, cougars, and wolves; Oh my! But you're far more likely to have an unpleasant encounter with bees on a trail ride. These industrious insects are quick to press an attack when they feel their home has been threatened. Be prepared to take swift action if you run into these creatures on a ride. The encounter won't be fun, but keeping your calm should help prevent any worse consequences.

See also Pests

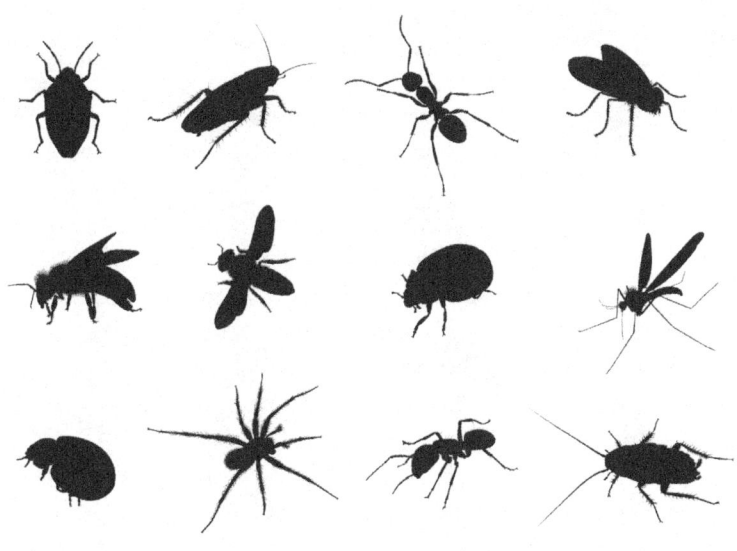

J

JOURNEY

Whether your ride is a quick excursion away from the office or a backcountry expedition, the experience of the activity is what keeps us exploring on the back of a willing beast. It's not necessarily the destination; it's getting there that's the best part.

I use our trailer door as a logbook of our journeys.

K

KNIFE

I'm a big believer in every horse owner having a sharp, easily accessible knife on them when they're around livestock. A blade is not just to cut baling twine, slice bacon, or whittle when you're bored. It could save lives; maybe yours.

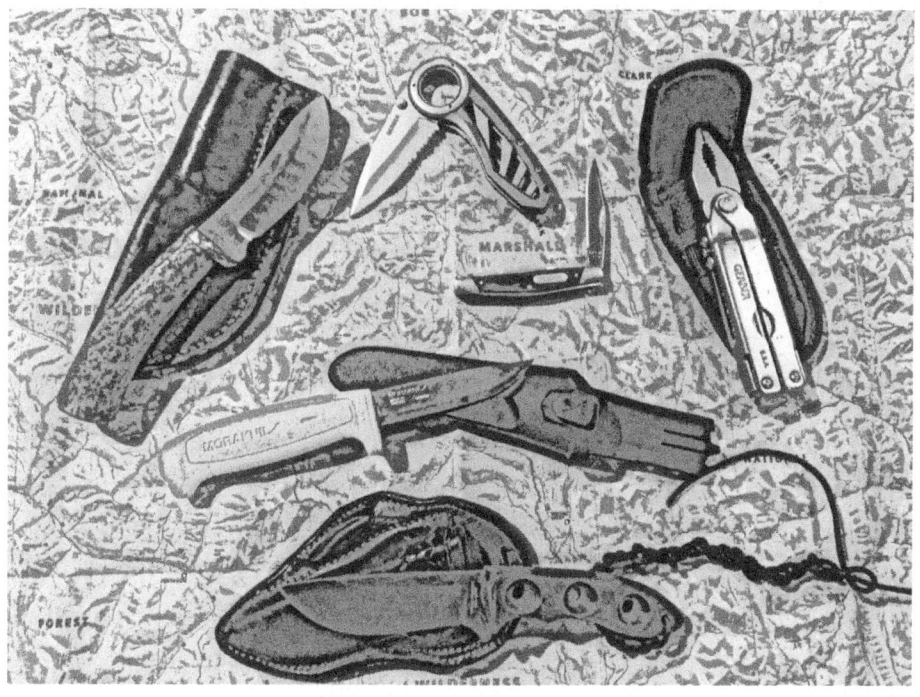

Knives are known to be one of the first tools ever invented. Even though a trail ride isn't typically a "survival" scenario, a knife is an essential tool for every rider heading into the great outdoors, whether it's around the back pasture, or around a Wilderness.

The following pages will discuss and describe what to look for in a dependable blade.

When do you most often use a knife? Here are my top four uses for a Knife.

1. Opening packets (of food).
2. Repairs.
3. Making a spark (with a fire steel).
4. Cutting rope.

These are all pretty mundane uses and typical reasons why we need a knife when we're on the trail, and they're all valid.

PRO TIP

One of the 10 essentials that every rider should carry on every ride is a very important tool: a knife.

But what type of knife?

I prefer a fixed blade knife that I carry on my belt. I like the blade to be about 3.5 to 4 inches long. Long enough to get to the bottom of the peanut butter jar! In an emergency, I can pull it out, not worry about opening a blade, and quickly handle whatever situation I'm in at the time.

There's also a place for a folding knife. The cowboys of yore nearly all carried a folding pocketknife. They were called "Stockmen's Knives" and usually had three blades. You may not cut yourself out of a wreck with one, but for opening a bag of Fritos, they're perfect! These useful tools are still available, and I usually have one in my pocket.

For quick repairs, a multi-tool calls my saddlebags home. Not only do they have a knife blade, one of the biggest pros of the multi-tool is undoubtedly the pliers. The entire tool is designed around them. Pliers are something people wind up needing a lot more than they think they will and being able to carry them with you is a huge bonus.

Fixed Blade Benefits
- Simple to use.
- No moving parts.
- Less opportunity to cut yourself. (With no need to disengage a locking mechanism and fold the blade, there is less opportunity to accidentally cut yourself in the process.)
- Easier to maintain.

Folding Knife Benefits
- No sheath required.
- Stores more compactly.
- Multi-use… If it's a multi-tool, you'll have additional gadgets in addition to the blade in one compact package.

Serrated or not?
Ropes today are often made of nylon or polypropylene, which can be hard to cut with an ordinary or plain blade. So, the serrated blade, or a partially serrated blade has become popular with many people.

Plain Blades: In general, a plain edge is best when doing push cuts. Also, the plain edge is superior when control, accuracy, and clean cuts are necessary.

- Push cuts: The main cutting is done by pushing the edge through the thing-to-be-cut. For example, when peeling an apple, you push the blade edge under the skin of the apple. When chopping wood, you try to push the edge into and through the wood.

Serrated Blades: In general, the serrated edge works better for slicing cuts, especially through hard or tough surfaces, where the serrations tend to grab and cut the surface easily.

- Slicing cuts: The cutting action is substantially done by dragging the edge across the thing-to-be-cut. When you slice a tomato, you drag the edge across the tomato as you cut through it. Slicing and sawing are examples of slicing cuts.

I feel naked when caught without a knife as it is the most basic of tools. I can cut baling twine, lash ropes, make a fire, and a million other uses. Heck, I even use my knife as a screwdriver at times. I urge you to find and carry a knife whenever you're around horses and mules. You'll wonder how you ever got around without one.

KNOTS
When you're camping with horses it's imperative to have some knowledge of knots. Handy in a multitude of situations from highlines to keep your ponies nearby overnight to trailer ties to keep them nearby while you saddle, every horse owner should know a few basic knots.

Experienced outdoor folks always end their knots with a slippery loop that releases quickly and easily even after being under load. The alternative is to pick, swear, and cut.

For horse folk, just a few knots are enough to get us out and back. I recommend the following as an excellent starting point; Bowline, Half Hitch, Prusik, and Trucker's Hitch.

I generally start, or anchor, the lines for highlines, tarps, and tents with a Bowline and end with a couple of Half Hitches. A Trucker's Hitch will get and hold a rope tight using a makeshift pulley and a little Archimedes principle.

See also Alpine Butterfly, Bowline, Gadgets, Half Hitch, Prusik, Trucker's Hitch

L

LATIGO

I get a lot of questions about why I don't use off billets, preferring instead to hang latigos on all four corners of my saddle. That is generally immediately followed with "why nylon?".

Most western-style saddles have rigging dees. They're the big, hefty rings placed around the saddle and those attachment points are what the cinch ultimately hangs from. Most saddles have a latigo (the long leather or nylon strap) on the near-side and an off billet (a shorter strap with holes in it) on the off-side. The rear dees generally have billets on both sides.

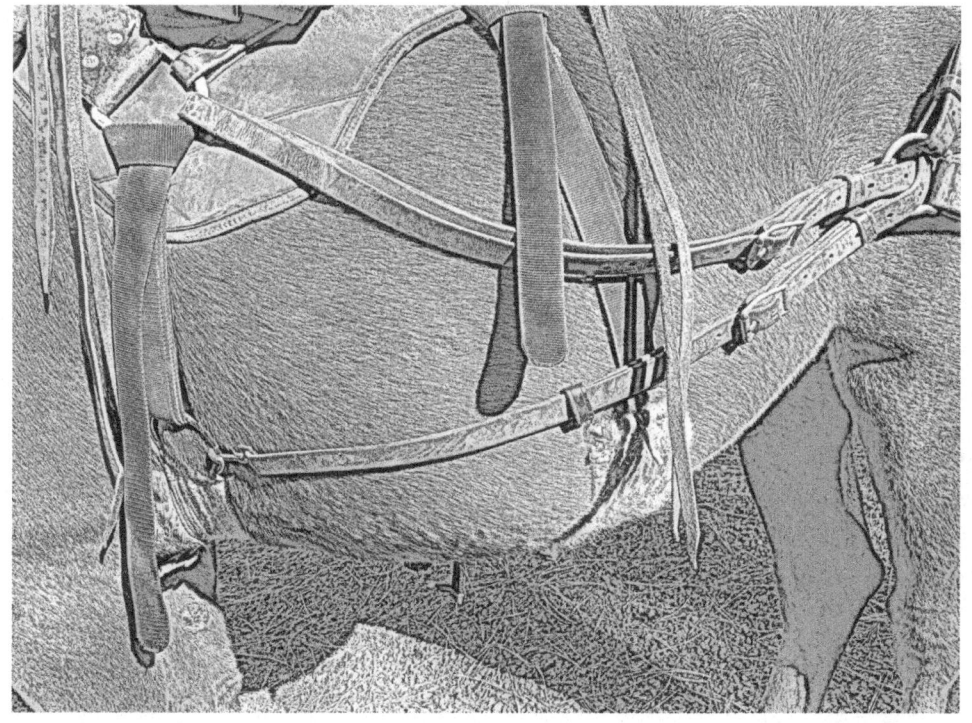

ABCs of Horse Camping

Latigo vs. Billets

I've removed every billet on every saddle I own and replaced them with latigos. By using latigos exclusively, I can easily make precise adjustments to the cinch's tightness from either side of the animal.

When riding, you may only have the offside to work on when adjusting a cinch. It's much easier to do that with a latigo. Additionally, the use of two latigos allows for an infinitely customized fit for my animals. Doing this keeps Ruger and the girls more comfortable, the saddles in place, and helps me stay safe, all of which are good things.

Nylon vs. Leather

The material for your latigos matters; it's what is holding your saddle on. I like nylon for the following reasons:

- It's easy to clean.
- Makes a smaller, more compact knot.

I dislike leather latigos for these reasons:

- Leather is slippery when wet.
- When cold, leather gets stiff.
- Leather requires regular maintenance.

The next time you're cleaning and oiling leather, consider nylon latigos. They're lighter than leather, more affordable than leather, and will last a lifetime.

LEAD ROPES

Used as an extension of your arm, these woven bits of fabric date back to prehistoric times and allow us to temporarily tie a pony, direct his movement, and much more.

Using this ubiquitous tool as an extension of your arm lets you work your animals safely.

Choosing the right lead rope involves more than choosing a color. The key things I consider when purchasing a lead line include:

Length – I prefer longer leads in the range of 12-15 feet. A longer lead allows me to work my animals at a greater distance with more subtle cues. 12 -15 feet allows me to toss the excess line over and around my animals with ease as I get them comfortable with ropes. It's worth mentioning that these longer ropes tend to puddle at your feet and can be a challenge for those who, like myself, have coordination issues! Find a length that works comfortably for you, not what someone is peddling as a magic cure-all.

Material – I love thick, soft cotton leads. They feel wonderful in your hand, like a warm hug on a cold day. I don't use them. On cold, wet days, the damp cotton quickly becomes unpleasant in the extreme. A much better material choice is yacht braid. The woven polyester construction is strong, defies water, and is easy on the hands.

Snap or Knot – How you connect the lead to the halter is an important consideration. My favorites forego breakage-prone hardware and use a simple knot or slip loop to connect the two pieces.

LIGHTWEIGHT HORSE CAMPING

Going on an overnight camping trip with your trail horse is simple with the right planning, especially for those already familiar with camping and backcountry riding. For many people camping with horses away from the trailhead evokes images of pack mules, canvas wall tents, and the delicious aroma of Dutch oven cooking wafting through a pine-scented meadow. While this is a beautiful image and a great way to experience the backcountry, here's a bit of hard truth. Most horse owners don't have the skills, or the pack animals, needed to haul in the hundreds of pounds of gear to make this picture a reality. There's an alternative: Lightweight horse camping directly off your riding stock.

I started lightweight horse camping shortly after I was introduced to backcountry Wilderness riding. Before I had a pack animal, I wanted to experience riding the high mountains without inviting myself on my friends' pack trips. They're great people, but sometimes you must go your own way.

At first blush, it may appear that a 1,000-pound beast could easily carry all your gear and his without issue. That would be wrong. The US Cavalry used 20% of the horse's weight as the maximum that it could carry. Let's do a little math, 20% of 1,000 pounds foots out to 200 pounds. In this example, 200 lbs. is your total weight allowance, including you, the weight of your saddle and tack, and your camp equipment. As you see, you'll run out of capacity quickly, sometimes before you get to the camping equipment!

I use 20% as a generalization, not a rule. I want to be as considerate as possible to my animals. Ruger and the girls come to the gate when they hear me hitching up the trailer. I want that behavior to continue, so it behooves me to be careful with their loads. Not only do I weigh every item the horse is carrying, but I also keep our days short, take frequent breaks, and even occasionally dismount and walk to give my animals a breather.

If you've done any backpacking, you already know some of the lightweight options available. If you haven't, it's time to look to the world of ultra-lightweight hiking for areas to reduce both weight and volume. For example, many ultra-lightweight sleeping bags weigh under 8 ounces. A trip through your local backpacking store can dramatically reduce your hard-working pony's load. Through careful selection, I've managed to reduce the weight of my camp and highline equipment to under 10 pounds. Food weight is another concern that we'll address next.

Lightweight horse camping is not the realm of romantic ideas of fine dining in the Wilderness. Robust meals of steak and potatoes are best enjoyed when you have multiple pack animals to haul them. Instead, look to freeze-dried and instant meals that require little more than the addition of hot water. Lightweight horse camping is about the journey and the adventure, not the comforts of home.

Your horse's meals when lightweight camping will be predicated on the availability of grazing. A saddle horse already burdened by the weight of you, your tack, camp, etc., won't have the carrying capacity to carry the hay or pellets he'll need. You'll have to plan your trip around good grazing and reliable water sources. You may be able to smuggle a few pounds of grain, but while these may be enough to get him through a lean night, they're not nearly enough for a multi-day trek. Prior planning is paramount for successful and pleasant lightweight horse camping.

Once you've determined where you're heading and what you'll be taking, it's time to figure out how to carry the load safely and efficiently. You'll find oversized  saddlebags in any tack shop. Don't use them. Large saddlebags encourage you to take more than you need and place the weight in the wrong place. Instead, use the smallest possible saddle and cantle bags for light but bulky items, such as sleeping bags and shelter. Use compression straps to reduce the volume of these items. Place heavier gear forward in your horn bags.

As you load your bags of gear, consider how you'll mount and dismount your horse. I've seen so-called "lightweight" horse campers who had difficulty swinging their legs past overfilled bags. Not being able to get your legs clear of your packs could have dangerous consequences. Carry only what is required, not everything that you'd like.

Be honest with yourself when considering what is essential and what is a luxury. A camp chair does wonders for an aching back but isn't required. You may get away with bringing a hearty steak for the first night's dinner, but does that indulgence give your hard-working horse a fair deal?

Carrying additional items that are nice but not required for health and safety may push you into the realm of packing. My quest for a more comfortable camp and better meals is what brought me into the world of packing and the acquaintance of many fine pack mules. Rather than overburden my saddle horse, I learned the art of packing, and you can too. Ellie and Cocoa now carry camp and all the extra's that make Wilderness horse camping a comfy highlight of my life.

Now that you've got some ideas for lightweight horse camping adventures, start your planning and preparations.

LOVE NOTES

Let the people that manage your riding locations know that horse owners are using these areas. Without letting them know equestrian activities are occurring, they may forget it when it comes to dedicating time, effort, and money to maintaining horse trails, equine parking, and horse camping areas.

We try to pen a quick note to the land manager of each area where we

ride or camp so that they are aware of the equine users in the places they are responsible. In conversations with various recreation rangers from around the continent, few have received "Thank you's". They've gotten many complaints, though.

Positive reinforcement works. Or as coined by Benjamin Franklin in his 1744 publication of Poor Richard's Almanac, "Tart words make no friends: A spoonful of honey will catch more flies than a gallon of vinegar."

Applying this phrase in our world of trail riding and horse camping is pretty simple: To get our public employees to perform at a higher level for our needs, you are more apt to succeed by utilizing positive reinforcement.

Get out those love letters and postcards and say thank you!

LOW IMPACT

Are you a ghost rider on the trail? You're only riding your horse to and from your trailer or camp spot, and Leave No Trace (LNT) only applies when we're camping, right? Wrong.

Leave No Trace principles are just as applicable to the recreational trail rider as the dedicated backcountry packer. The actions of those of us that ride in the "front country" may have more impact due to the greater number of users.

We get so much enjoyment from trail riding that we should take every opportunity to make sure that trail restrictions do not increase and threaten our ability to ride on our favorite trails. As equestrian trail users, we have many opportunities to protect our trails. We can take steps before we leave the barn, before we saddle up, and when we arrive back at camp or trailer. These simple and easy tips will help.

Before the ride – Before we take the first step on the trail, we'll start minimizing our impact by planning for the ride.

Choose your trail wisely – Save rides in historically wet or muddy areas for times when conditions are typically drier. The object is to "Leave No Trace", and a horse on muddy or marshy ground is going to leave holes and churned mud. The whole idea of LNT is that no one will know you've been there.

Practice at home – Make a point of crossing water, logs, and other obstacles during your regular rides. A horse that fights his rider at a stream crossing is not only dangerous but tramples the bank and pushes sediment into the water. Backcountry horses, and riders, need to be trained not only for rider safety but also to protect the environment.

Know your route and how to "Stay Found". Getting lost causes undue damage to the land and considerable risk for rescuers. Carry and know how to use a map.

During the ride – Once we get on the trail, opportunities to reduce our impact grow even larger.

Travel on durable surfaces and stay on the trail. Don't go around  muddy areas should you come across them. Train your horse to go straight through. If you go around muddy spots, the trail will widen and become even muddier in the future. Mud is part of the trail riding experience. Expect it.

Refrain from cutting switchbacks or shortcuts. After waiting all week to go trail riding, why take a shortcut just to get back quicker?

Horse hooves exert pressures exceeding 1,000 pounds per square inch, which makes the destructive potential from horses significant. We can reduce this by taking the following steps.

Stay in the center of the trail, single file, and avoid trailside vegetation areas. The one thousand plus pounds of pressure that a horse places on the land could quickly trample and destroy off-trail areas.

Don't let your horse stop on the trail to make a deposit. Keep the horse moving, and the manure will naturally scatter behind, speeding up decomposition and causing less bother for other trail users.

Pack out everything that you packed in. How does a 12 oz. can of your favorite beverage weigh more when empty than full? If you take it out, bring it back. This shared failing of all trail users is easily corrected. Keep our trails clean and enjoyable for years to come by simply "Packing it out".

Pack "it" out – Dispose of all waste properly, including your own. It boils down to one simple thing "Pack it in-Pack it out". There is no reason ever to see "Trail Daisies". Pommel bags can carry personal gear such as an emergency kit, lunch, and a bathroom kit—a re-sealable plastic bag with toilet paper, a small folding shovel, and other necessities. Follow Leave No Trace techniques to dispose of human waste properly.

Taking Breaks – Not only can we be model trail users during our ride, but we should also extend this to our rest stops and breaks from the trail.

Take rest breaks well off the trail on durable surfaces such as dry grass, sand, or rocks.

Tying to Trees – You should only tie horses to trees for short periods of time. Select a live tree at least 8" in diameter. To prevent most of the damage that a rope can do to the bark, wrap the lead rope around the trunk at least twice before tying it off. Also, teach your horse to tie and stand patiently. A horse that paws while tied will compact the soil, which not only leaves an unsightly ring but might damage or kill the tree. If you have an intractable pawer, bring hobbles.

Practice "Leave Negative Trace" by leaving the trail in a BETTER condition than you found it. If you see an old can on the side of the trail, pick it up and pack it out. Pick up any trash you find along the trail. A little preventative maintenance will make a big difference. Bits of trash, such as soda and beer cans, cigarette butts, candy wrappers, twist ties, etc., are common trail eyesores and should all be packed out.

As our preferred mode of transportation becomes more and more common, equestrian trail users are asked to minimize their trail impact by means such as those used by hikers. By demonstrating our concern for trails as a sustainable resource, horse riders can become leaders in LNT advocacy and in protecting our continued ability to ride in our favorite places.

PRO TIP

Be a GOOD equine ambassador.

Be a Ghost Rider on the Trail.

ABCs of Horse Camping

MAPS

When I first ventured out of the arena and onto the trails, I used whatever navigational tools were readily available. Sometimes they were OK, and often they weren't, but for the most part, I was able to get back to the trailhead…eventually.

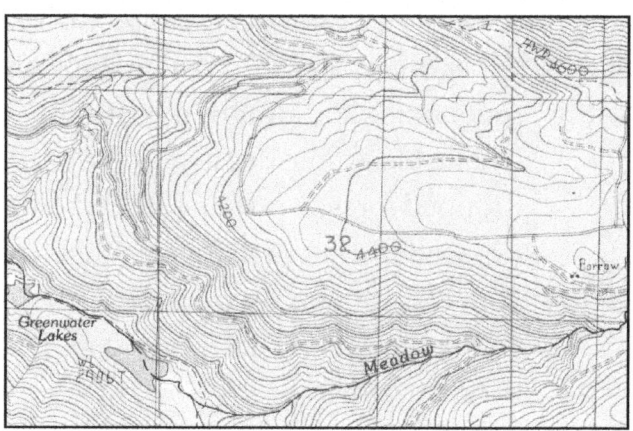

When I started exploring the high mountains, I frequently had to create my own navigational tools assembled from various sources. Regardless of where you ride, having a reliable trail map, and knowing how to use it is imperative. Here's more info on what types of maps I carry and why to ensure that I get home in time for dinner.

Physical vs. Digital

On almost every ride, I carry three types of topographic trail maps. Two of these will be physical paper maps: an overview small-scale map and a detailed large-scale map. I'll also generally have a set of digital maps loaded on my phone or GPS. Each of these tools adds to the functionality of the others.

Despite the seeming preponderance of digital gadgets that I see on the trail, traditional paper maps are simply better than digital. Consider these four reasons.

1) They offer a significantly larger viewing window: an 11-by-17-inch map amounts to 187 square inches of topographic detail, or nearly 20 times larger than the screen on my iPhone.
2) Paper maps can be written on, which is useful for making route notes and drawing bearings.
3) Unlike electronic devices, there's little to no impact if a map is dropped or sat on, and they remain functional after being exposed to water (so long as they've been waterproofed).
4) Paper maps don't require batteries or recharging, and they're easily viewed by multiple people together when discussing the daily ride.

I won't deny that the appeal of digital maps is real, and these tools certainly have their place in your gear list. GPS units, and smartphones, slide into pockets and require no laborious folding. Also, depending upon the app, these digital devices can reliably pinpoint your location in an instant without much work or thought involved. A lack of thoughtfulness is not necessarily a good thing.

Overview (small-scale) Maps

Overview maps normally have a scale of between 1:50,000 and 1:100,000, meaning that one unit on the map (e.g., an inch, a centimeter, a thumbnail) equals 50,000 or 100,000 units in the field. They usually cover a defined area, like a national park or wilderness area, where the entire trip will take place.

When planning a trip, I use these small-scale maps to develop a general understanding of the landscape, including the main watersheds and trail networks. They help plot general routes and evaluate potential alternates.

On the trail, overview maps are helpful for pinpointing distant landmarks and serve as a reference for midtrip route discussions, detours, and self-evacuations if needed.

Small-scale maps can work for on-trail navigating. However, by definition, the topographic detail on a small-scale map is compressed, making it challenging to associate features on the map with features in the field, particularly subtle ones. If your map-reading skills leave something to be desired (be honest), trying to improve them using small-scale maps will generate limited results.

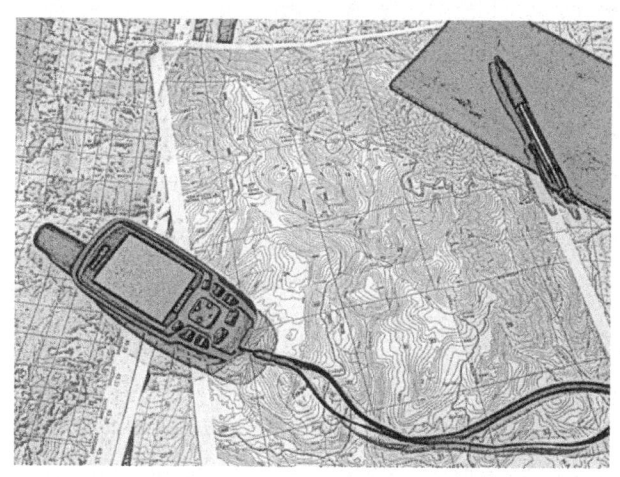

Making matters worse, most overview maps do not use a standard scale or contour intervals, so you have to relearn these relationships with every map. For example, I use an overview map of Montana's Bob Marshall complex with a 1:80,000 scale and 100-foot contour lines. In contrast, the map I use in the Pasayten Wilderness in Washington is scaled at 1:50,000 with 50-foot contour lines, making the topography appear steeper. When I go from one area to the other, I have to remember the map differences.

Detail (large-scale) Maps

When planning a trip, I use very detailed large-scale maps to plan my route precisely. I rely on them for navigation and to find campsites and water sources. A large-scale map is one in which an area is "zoomed in" on the map.

The gold standard for large-scale maps is a digitized series, produced by the US Forest Service (USFS) and accessed digitally, using platforms like CalTopo and /or GaiaGPS. USFS, and US Geological Survey (USGS), maps can be exported out of CalTopo and Gaia into print-ready PDFs. I'm a fan of 11-by-17-inch printouts.

Digital Maps

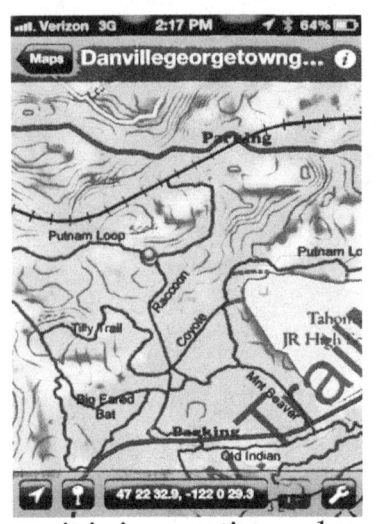

As a backup and supplement to my paper maps, I also load digital maps onto my smartphone or GPS unit. These digital maps have value, even aside from the software they bring. If I lose my paper maps or get way off route (both have happened), digital maps quickly become invaluable.

Regardless of where you ride, having a reliable trail map, and knowing how to use it is imperative unless you're a fan of being late for dinner.

Maps – Topographic

Have you ever looked closely at the squiggly lines scattered over your topo maps? Besides the obvious trails and rivers, the brown squiggly lines are contour lines. These fascinating lines represent the three-dimensional landscape of Earth within the two-dimensional confines of a map. Contour lines give us 3-D glasses.

Topographic trail maps are useful for trip planning and for navigation in the field. They give you the power to visualize three-dimensional terrain from a flat piece of paper.
See also Contour lines

PRO TIP
Many overview maps have shaded relief. The shading causes features to stand out but can play tricks on your eyes. Use care when using these.

MUD

When trails tend to be muddy during the shoulder seasons, it's a good idea to find a different area to ride if possible. Know which trails get muddy and seek out drier areas. If you're stuck on a muddy trail, ride straight through those muddy stretches. Skirting mucky spots or taking shortcuts widens the trail tread, hastens erosion, and scars the landscape with a maze of "social trails". If your animal doesn't want to go through mud and water? Congratulations! You've just found a hole in his education and a new training opportunity.
See also Low Impact, Training

N

NAVIGATION SKILLS

Before heading onto the trails of your dreams, be confident in your ability to return to camp well in time for dinner. At a minimum, be able to read and understand a topographic map. Know how a compass works. Be familiar with any electronic route-finding tools you may be carrying. If you count on your horse to know the way home, eventually, you'll spend more time hungry and afoot than you'd like.

See also Compass, Contour Lines, Declination, Essentials, GPS, Maps

NEARSIDE NONSENSE

Horse riders are traditionally taught to mount from the left or near side of the horse. Since you never know what obstacles might present themselves, you should be able to get in and out of the saddle equally well from both sides of your riding animal.

O

OBSTACLES

Most riders eventually progress beyond the groomed bridle paths of suburbia to wilder areas that are home to various obstacles ranging from downed trees and stream crossings to hikers and bicyclists. Teach yourself and your horse how to handle these hurdles before you get too far from home.

As a trail rider, YOU are a high-performance athlete, and your horse is your high-performance partner. By high performance, I'm not referring to the various "extreme trail riding" events we often see. We are doing high-level riding away from judges, spectators, and crowds and asking a lot from our horses and ourselves as active trail riders.

So, what does "high performance" mean if not competing for time in an arena course filled with obstacles that bear little resemblance to the world outside? Let's examine some of the obstacles you may encounter; without pool noodles and no timers to race against.

Bridges - If we want to go any distance, we're either riding on bridges or fording streams. I ride short animals and dislike getting wet so having my mount comfortable with bridges is a must.

Water Crossings - Of course, bridges aren't always an option, and we  may have to take a wetter route to get to the next trail challenge or your campsite for the night.

Water crossings are often a source of contention between riders and their animals, which is why they are so commonly seen in trail competitions. In the real world, that thin blue line on the map has the potential to be the biggest challenge and potential danger of the trip.

Logs - All the water we've previously had to negotiate helps grow trees, lots of trees, with branches that fall onto the trail. Some of these branches are natural cavaletti that nature provides to remind our mounts to watch their feet. Others have more in common with the jumps found on an eventing course. Get off your horse and remove them. Downfall is an excellent reason to carry a pack saw; it's called trail maintenance. As equestrians, we share the trails with many other users, and one of the best ways to help keep this access is to help maintain the trails that we enjoy.

Rocks - The water that grows such large trees also washes off a lot of the dirt that once covered the rocky bones of the mountains. Stones big and small remind your horse to watch his step and maintain balance.

Manmade Obstacles - Any obstacle course worth its salt will also feature an artificial challenge or two, and the trail into the wilderness is no exception. Many of the trails we use are shared with hikers and bicyclists. Acclimatizing ourselves and our mounts to handle and accept these tests is sometimes the most challenging thing about trail riding. From a biker swiftly and silently approaching to the hiker with a horse-eating fishing pole waving about, these real-world obstacles are common and should be addressed before we venture forth on the trails.

See also Training, Water Crossing Training

The sign reads:

BIG CROW BASIN
NORSE PEAK TR. 1191
PACIFIC CREST 2000

P

PACKING

Packing is the science, or art, of moving materials from one point to another using horses or mules as the means of conveyance. These skills are not learned overnight but take study and practice.

Many trail riders love the idea of packing their camping gear onto a horse for an epic trip into the backcountry. Then they're dazed with the mysteries of the diamond hitch, overcome with tales of remarkable wrecks, and been told that packing is a dark art that takes a lifetime to master. Don't believe it.

You can learn all the primary packing skills. Years of mastery of the art, though a worthy goal, isn't necessary for a safe, enjoyable trip up the trail to your backcountry camp. Find a reliable mentor to guide you on your journey.

PERSONAL LOCATOR BEACONS

PLB's are the land-based equivalents of Emergency Position Indicating Radio Beacons (EPIRBs), a sea-going technology that has been in use for decades. These devices are high-powered (usually 5 watts) and designed to send out an emergency distress signal. With a PLB, it's very important to remember that they should only be activated in situations of grave and imminent danger.

- PLB devices communicate with a network of military satellites that relay your information to a US Air Force Rescue Coordination Center who determines the type and scope of response necessary and coordinates with federal, state, and local officials to affect your immediate rescue. When using a GPS-compatible PLB in the continental US, it takes only minutes to alert search-and-rescue personnel of your position.

- PLB's have a higher upfront cost when compared to Satellite Messengers. While prices for PLB's are coming down, these units still typically cost more than a Satellite Messenger with costs ranging from $300 to $500.
- No Ongoing Fees. Unlike Satellite Messengers, Personal Locator Beacons do not require you to pay any recurring subscription fees for the device to work as designed. Some new Personal Locator Beacons offer an optional, subscription service, that allows the user to send an email or text message that includes your location information. This feature is a way to keep family and friends informed.

- PLB's are equipped with a long-lasting lithium battery. The batteries remain dormant until you flip the switch to activate the PLB and will power the device for 24 hours. These are not user-replaceable and must be installed by a manufacturer-certified replacement center. PLB batteries are designed to last for five years before replacement.

To me, a PLB is about calling in the troops when the "stuff" really hits the fan.

See also Communications, Satellite Messengers

PESTS

It's a fact. Bugs are part of the great outdoors, and many a trail ride has become a nightmare of slapping, scratching, and even swearing because of pests. Sometimes it seems that the entire insect kingdom is out to make us and our animals miserable.

Wherever we ride, we'll encounter insect pests of some type. Here's the low down on the five most common biting and stinging pests that you'll encounter, when you'll find them, and how to fight them.

Mosquitoes

The mosquito is the deadliest animal family in the world. It might seem impossible that something so small can kill so many people, but it's true. According to the World Health Organization, mosquito bites result in the deaths of more than 1 million people every year.

When you'll find them: Some species bite all day long, some are most active at sunup and sundown, and others feed in the cooler hours between dusk and dawn.

Diseases they carry: West Nile virus (WNV), malaria, yellow fever, Chikungunya, dengue fever, and Zika virus.

Fight them with: Products containing DEET.
QUICK FACT – Only female mosquitoes bite.

Sand Flies/Black Flies
Wet areas throughout the north are home to these nuisances whose populations swell from April to July.

When you'll find them: These flies usually bite during the day in outdoor shaded or partially shaded areas

Diseases they carry: Vesicular stomatitis (VS), a viral disease that affects both horses and humans. Equine symptoms are fever, mouth sores, and face-rubbing; humans typically develop flu-like symptoms.

Fight them with: Products containing DEET or picaridin are most effective. Given the limited effectiveness of repellents, protecting oneself against biting flies requires taking additional measures. Avoid wet areas inhabited by the flies, avoid peak biting times, and wear heavy-duty, light-colored clothing, including long-sleeve shirts, long pants, and hats.

QUICK FACT – Black flies are attracted to mammals by the carbon dioxide in exhaled breath as well as dark colors.

Horseflies & Deer Flies

Large and agile in flight these ferocious breeds of flies have cutting and tearing mouthparts that are capable of easily piercing a shirt. Their painful bites can make a normally calm horse lose control.

When you'll find them: In the daytime. They prefer to fly in sunlight, avoiding dark and shady areas.

Diseases they carry: Equine infectious anemia (EIA), biting flies can transfer EIA from horse to horse.

Fight them with: Most repellents don't impress these hard-hitting flies.

QUICK FACT – Horseflies have appeared in literature since 465 BC when the Greek playwright Aeschylus mentioned them driving people to madness through their persistent pursuit.

Bees – Wasps – Hornets

Encountering bees is not pleasant, but if you keep your wits about you, and leave the area quickly, you should be all right.

When you'll find them: Throughout the summer but especially autumn, these territorial insects will become more aggressive than usual as the days grow shorter. Wasp/hornet nests and beehives may be found in dead/hollow trees and logs hanging from tree branches. Nests may also be in the ground or dug into the stream banks. When riled, any exposed area of your horse's body (and yours) is fair game.

Fight them with: Insect repellents don't work against these stinging insects. Instead, awareness and avoidance are your best bet. Keep an eye out for nests and hives. Be ready to shout. If you're on the trail and your horse is stung, shout "BEES!" to warn other riders. Before you head out talk with your ride partners about what to do if you encounter bees on the trail.

QUICK FACT – Yellowjackets are sometimes mistakenly called "bees" (as in "meat bees"), given that they are similar in size and both sting, but they are actually wasps.

Ticks

These small arachnids have incisor-like claws that can tunnel beneath your skin in seconds.

When you'll find them: Ticks are widespread from spring until after the year's first killing frost.

They particularly like to attach to the base of your horse's mane and tail, to the insides of his ears, and inner thighs.

Diseases they carry: Ticks are implicated in the transmission of a number of infections, notably Lyme disease which both you and your horse are vulnerable. Other gifts from the tick include typhus, Rocky Mountain spotted fever, Colorado tick fever, tularemia, babesiosis, and ehrlichiosis.

Fight them with: Constant awareness (inspect yourself and your horse closely and often, several times per day). Prompt, careful removal is key. Some repellents have proven to be helpful. Especially permethrin, which when applied to clothes, repels and kills ticks for months. DEET has been shown to repel ticks, but mainly at higher concentrations (upward of 20 percent). Research has found that the repellant picaridin works pretty well against ticks.

QUICK FACT – The fossil record suggests ticks have been around at least 90 million years.

PLANNING A BACKCOUNTRY CAMPING TRIP

Riding and horse camping is the ultimate way to experience the world on horseback. When you're exploring new areas, it pays to be prepared.

Knowing what to expect beforehand will help you decide what to take and help if your plans unexpectedly change. After all, you can't jump in your car to resolve a rainy-day tent failure or a minor medical emergency when you're 20 miles from the trailhead. Here are our basic guidelines to prepare for overnight treks into remote areas.

1 - Try a Practice Run at Home

Test any new equipment before your trip. Learn how to set up that new tent at home and try out new saddles and tack before you leave.

Before you visit a new area, take a few rides with the same equipment that you'll take on your trip. It's better to adjust things at home than on the fly. Taking a few rides with an actual load before your trip will help you gauge your and your animal's fitness for the adventure.

2 - Do the Research

Now is the time to start learning about an area to see if it fits your plans. I always start with an online search where a few quick clicks will return information about potential horse camping areas. Use **www.TrailMeister.com** for info on what to expect at a given area, including pictures, accurate directions to the trailhead, trail maps of the site, weather, links to land managers, and even GPS tracks.

Know the Weather and Terrain

A major factor to consider is the forecast and season. You need to pack and prepare for just about any weather, and it's important to have realistic expectations before you go.

- Check a topographic map to see what altitudes you'll encounter. Remember that the weather may vary widely with elevation. A warm summer day at 700 feet can be a snowy wonderland at 7,000.
- Make a mental note of your expected route and destination point. How far will you be from your truck or base camp? Will you be riding a loop or an out and back route? What are alternate routes to take in the event that Plan A fails and you need a Plan B?
- Check the type of terrain you'll encounter. Will there be ample grazing and water for your animals? Is it open space, heavily forested, or marshy?

Know the Rules

Knowing an area's regulations beforehand will make your trip much smoother.

- Are permits required?
- Are there fire restrictions?
- Are there bear restrictions?

3 - Pack Right

Most of what you'll take will be determined by your destination, length of trip, and what type of weather you'll likely encounter. Your equipment should be as practical, comfortable, and as lightweight as possible. Your horse will thank you! Quality gear

comes at a premium, but the pounds not carried are worth their weight in gold.

Organize gear into two groups: human and equine.

Human Needs

- Clothing – Jacket, stocking cap and gloves, camp shoes, insulating layers, etc.
- Shelter – Tent / hammock, sleeping pad, sleeping bag, etc.
- Cooking – Cookstove and fuel, pots, cooking utensils, cup, water filter, etc.
- Emergency/10 Essentials – Remember to keep the 10 Essentials on your person in case you separate from your riding animal. Take a few extra days of any medications you need.

Equine Needs

- Saddles and tack - Make sure that all equipment fits well and is in good repair.
- Panniers – Options include hard boxes that can deter a hungry bear to soft bags that are more forgiving to your pack animals. Regardless of the type, balance is everything, so be sure to load with the same weight and volume on each side.

- Containment Options – There are several good options for keeping your animals in one place during your trip. I use all three. Before using any of these techniques in the backcountry make sure to get your horses used to them at home first.
  - Highline – The gold standard. A strong rope strung between two sturdy trees protected by tree savers will ensure that you'll be riding instead of walking the following morning.
  - Hobbles – Will nearly immobilize your horse. At first. Where grazing is permitted hobbles are an excellent way to allow your animals to graze while under your strict supervision.
  - Electric Fencing – Another method to allow your animals to graze and relax while under supervision. Electric fencing is not a substitute for a highline. Your animals may believe in the bite of the fence, but the local elk or deer population doesn't, and they are apt to bolt and tear down the thin line if you're not careful.
- Equine First Aid Kit – Check with your veterinarian for suggestions about what to take and how to treat minor issues.

Additionally, if you're in bear country, you want to carry bear spray. It's better to have it and not need it than the alternative.

And one last thing: There may be no bathrooms. Bring biodegradable toiletries. Don't forget a trowel or shovel for digging catholes.

4 - Sleep Setup
The old boy scout motto "Be Prepared" still holds true. Being prepared for sleeping in various conditions is not an exception. Your

sleeping gear must be matched for the weather conditions in the area that you plan to camp.

- A three-season tent is fine for most camping trips.
- A sleeping pad is essential. Not only does a pad add comfort, but most importantly, it provides insulation from the ground.
- Regarding sleeping bags, it's fair to say you should find one that is temperature-rated below what you expect.

When embarking on a multi-day trip in the backcountry, a certain level of discomfort is to be expected. Prepare your mind for this and embrace it. Sleeping in the backcountry will never be as comfortable as a night at the Ritz, but it can be quite pleasant with proper planning and the right equipment. It's a necessary skill to master for those wanting to head away from the beaten path. Ride hard enough, and a bed of granite and tree roots will feel like a pillowtop mattress.

5 – Meal Planning

Whether it's a quick overnight trip or a multi-day adventure, you want meals that will nourish and strengthen you and taste really good! You'll also want to factor in meals for your animals. Here are some quick ideas and common questions about meal planning for backcountry trips.

- How long will you be out? Factor in the meals you'll eat at the trailhead before and after your trip.

- What is the size of your group? Meals may be much simpler if you're going solo. If you're camping with others, decide if you want to share meals. A larger group can split the weight of food as well as fuel and cookware.

- What's on the menu? It helps to make a meal plan to know how much food to take. This could be as simple as writing it out on paper; or as complex as creating a spreadsheet. Start with dinners, which generally are the biggest meals of the day and the ones you're likely to sit down for.

- Test out recipes at home: Just as it's good practice to test out your stove or tent at home first, try potential camping recipes before you leave. Although food magically tastes better in camp, practice will give you an idea of how much preparation is required, cooking time, and adjustments you might want to make for taste.

- Feeding the ponies in backcountry areas: Horses require 2% of their body weight per horse per day for feed. Given the quantities required, you won't easily be able to take enough feed for your animals. Instead, you'll have to allow time during the day for your animals to graze. Portable electric fences are good options.

If you're camping in bear country, remember that smelly things (including toothpaste) may attract unwanted attention. A point about food that is often overlooked is that all kinds of animals raid food, not just bears. If your food supply is picked through by rodents or raccoons, it could be a trip-ender. For that reason, we always store our food in bear canisters.

Like most outdoor adventures, you need to be ready to change your plans. Mother nature doesn't care if you traveled hundreds of miles for your backcountry trip. Neither should you let that factor into your decision-making. Try to remember that it's not a failure if everything doesn't go according to your plan. Improvise as much as needed and have a good time camping! One of the many appeals of backcountry rides is the challenge they represent and the memories that remain afterward.

See also Essentials, Lightweight Horse Camping

PONYING

The art of leading another horse while you're mounted is a skill that

both you and your horse need to know. Ponying a young horse alongside a more experienced trail mount is a wonderful way to introduce him to the sights and experiences that he'll eventually experience on his own.

Put simply, ponying is the act of leading a horse from the animal you're riding. It sounds simple, but it's a multifaceted job of riding your horse while also paying attention to another, all while holding the reins in one hand and a lead rope in the other.

> **PRO TIP**
>
> **Learning to safely pony will help you when it's time to venture into the world of back country camping and wilderness trips.**

Why would anyone want to do this? Here are a few examples:

- Introduce a new horse to the trail.
- Lead a pack horse.
- Assist another rider.
- Condition a young or older horse.

In each of the preceding cases, you'll need to know how to pony properly to keep you, your horse, and the ponied horse safe.

Preparing You

Being ready to pony means that you need to be comfortable with the various tasks required of ponying another horse. Get used to riding your animal one-handed. Be able to rein with either hand while holding the lead in the other. Be able to switch hands on the go.

Preparing your Riding Animal
Before attempting to lead another animal, your riding horse should be comfortable with having a rope all around him. He needs to be OK with feeling a lead rope alongside his hindquarters, and even for the possibility that the rope might get around a leg or under his tail.

When I'm working with my animals, I constantly toss the lead rope around their hips and along their legs. I do this from all sides, left, right, front, and back. Once you can do that from the ground, it's time to try the same exercises from the saddle.

Your riding animal should calmly allow ropes to touch his legs and tail. He should also be able to drag logs without spooking. You don't have to be a professional roper, and a lariat isn't necessary. Just swing a lead rope to accustom your horse to the motions on both sides. Be careful.

I feel that rope training is an essential exercise for every animal. Your riding animal needs to be responsive and not afraid of a rope rubbing on it.

Preparing the Horse to be Led

It's my opinion that every trail horse should be able to be ponied. There are many reasons why, but my most significant is that if you depart your ride unexpectedly (say in a helicopter), your riding partner should be able to pony your horse back to the trailhead safely.

Start from the ground before you start leading from another horse. The horse you plan on ponying should be able to be led and led well from the ground before you try it from the saddle. Once the pony horse prospect has good ground manners and is light and alert at the end of a lead rope, transitioning to ponying won't be traumatic. Work from the ground until your prospect is consistent and responsive from a distance.

This groundwork not only will prepare your horse to be led from horseback, but it will also help him become a better and more respectful partner that doesn't pull or crowd you. Both are good things.

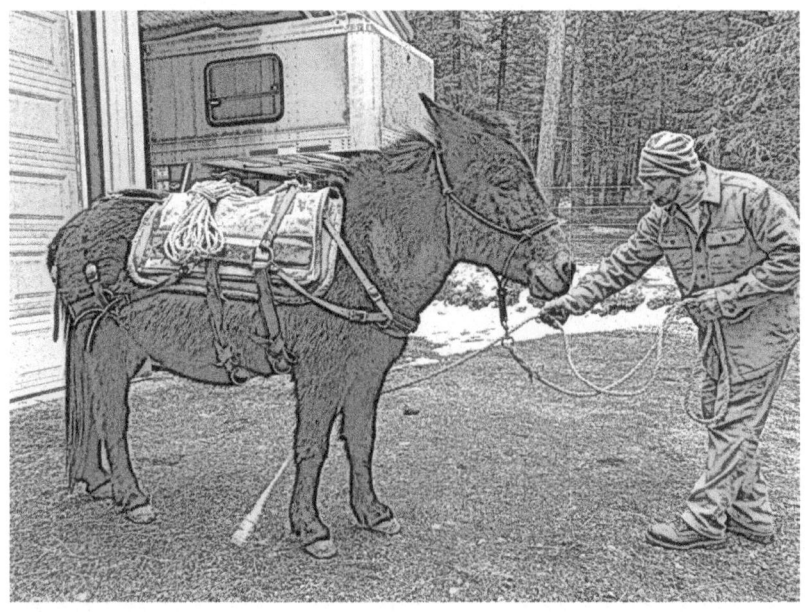

Essential Ponying Equipment

- Functional saddle with a solid tree – treeless or flexible tree saddles can deform and unevenly distribute pressure causing pain to your riding horse.
- Rope halter for the horse to be ponied – The rope halter will reinforce your cues.
- 12-foot lead – I've used both shorter and longer leads. 12 feet works best for me.
- Gloves – Rope burn is a thing and it's not pleasant.

The Dally

Once the three of you (your riding horse, the horse to be ponied, and yourself) have learned to pony safely and you're ready to head out, you'll be tempted to use your saddle horn. Don't. Use the horn to hold lunch, not tie off your lead rope. Should a ride become eventful while ponying, you want to be able to release all connections to the pony horse instantly. It's much better to dismount and pick up the lead than to be dragged off the side of a mountain because you were hard tied to an animal that lost its footing.

Successful ponying is dependent upon the response and respect you develop on the ground. If your horse handles well and is responsive on the ground, that training will come through when you pony him. Take the time to develop those skills.

PRUSIK

A prusik is a loop of cord that is wrapped around a rope to serve as a connection point. They can slide along the rope easily but lock tight when weighted.

The same features that allow the Prusik to be used to great effect by climbers ascending a mountain make it perfect for equestrian usage, especially when setting up a highline to secure your horses and mules overnight.

A Prusik is a friction hitch commonly seen and used extensively in climbing, mountaineering, and high-angle rope rescue. Anyplace there is a want for a strong and secure loop that will slide when needed is a good place to use a Prusik.

The term Prusik is a name for both the loops of cord and the hitch, and the verb is "to Prusik".

Steps to tying the Prusik:
1) Pass the cord around the rope and through itself as shown.
2) Pass the cord around the rope and through itself again.
3) Make at least three wraps around the rope, pull the cord tight. Make sure the wraps are neat.
4) When tension is removed, the loop can slide along the rope by pushing it down the length of the rope.

See also Knots, Highline

ABCs of Horse Camping

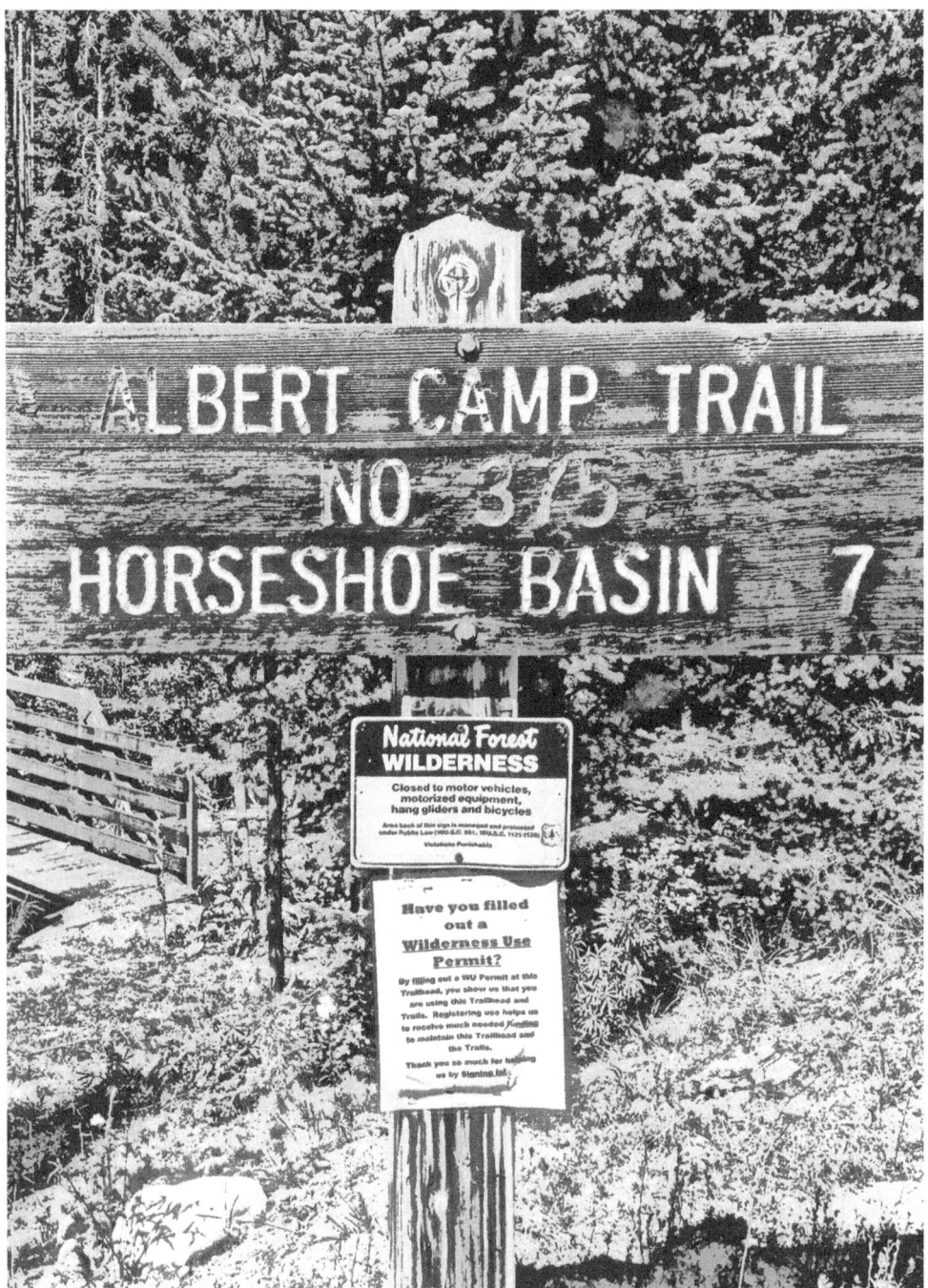

℧

QUICK RELEASE

Experienced outdoor folk always end their knots with a slippery loop that releases quickly and easily even after being under load. The alternative is to pick, swear, and cut. In the case of a panicked or trapped beast, a knot that quickly releases with a firm pull on the end of the rope is a very desirable trait.

Many knots have a "slippery hitch" variation that come apart in an instant. The quick-release knot's ability to provide an "emergency exit" is the reason they are valued as the knot of choice for safely tying horses.

See also Bowline

R

RESPONSIBLE TRAIL USE

If you're new to trail riding, it's easy to view it as just a hillier extension of the arena. It's just trail riding. Not quite. Trail riding offers an escape to beautiful, wild places — but also brings with it a responsibility to keep those places pristine and to respect other visitors' experiences. Here are a few tips to help you become an upstanding citizen of the trails.

Accept Responsibility

Personal responsibility has always been part of the equestrian ethic, whether it's just a day ride or an extended backcountry adventure.

Before heading onto the trails, learn about the area, gather the appropriate equipment, and be prepared to take care of yourself. Whether you're day riding or camping in backcountry areas for days on end, things could go wrong. Not only could you be in danger, but other people may have to shoulder the challenge of

bailing you out of trouble. A well-executed trip is a satisfaction to you and not a burden to others.

Respect Other Users

We're all members of one big trail family seeking quality experiences. We must learn to share. Our motivations are no different from those of other trail users regardless of our mode of travel. Here are my top three ways that we can show other users the respect they deserve.

Pick up your horse's poop ... at the trailhead

 Having an equine doesn't give you priority over other people's enjoyment of the trails or the trailhead. Recognize that everyone has the right to enjoy the outdoors. Please don't leave manure lying around the trailhead. Yes, it's grass. It's also a congestion point with many people and animals in one spot. A poo-filled parking area gives the impression that horsemen are slobs and gives credence to arguments that equine use should be restricted.

Know who has right of way ... with common sense

Basic traffic guidelines keep things moving smoothly and safely on the trails. When going downhill, yield to those coming up. Yes, mountain bikers and hikers should yield to equestrians, although, in practice, it can often be easier to let them go by. Yielding means establishing communication, being prepared to stop if necessary, and passing safely. A friendly "howdy" goes a long way!

Be a good dog ... owner

Dogs can leave their mark on the outdoors, in more ways than one. Responsible dog owners obey the rules, which differ from area to area. Are dogs allowed on the trail? Do they need to stay on a leash? Keep off-leash dogs in sight and under voice control to keep them from stressing wildlife or other trail users who don't like being jumped on, barked at, or attacked.

Protect the Environment

Trail riding and horse camping mean spending time in the great outdoors. Being prepared for those adventures means that you're going to hear the phrase "Leave No Trace" as often as you hear "Ten Essentials". What does it mean? Simply put, it's the best practices we should follow to enjoy and protect our natural spaces.

Here are my top four ways to help protect the trails and areas that we love.

1) Stay on that muddy trail. Ride straight through those muddy stretches of trail, and don't cut switchbacks. Skirting mucky spots or taking shortcuts widens the tread, hastens erosion, and scars the landscape with a maze of "social trails". Avoid mud with a bit of planning. Know which trails get muddy and simply seek out drier areas if possible.

2) Don't litter. Pack out all your trash and make an effort to pick up whatever garbage you find along the way. Yes, this may require you to dismount. It's good exercise, enjoy it.

3) Honor trail restrictions. Seasonal closures and other rules might keep you temporarily off your favorite trail, but they're in place for good reasons, like reducing erosion and protecting wildlife populations.

4) Give back - Horse Trails don't just happen. Although equestrians can be credited with developing many of the nation's earliest trails, the fact is today; horse riders must work to protect the access that used to be a given. Our theme song used to be "Home, Home on the Range". The tune has changed to "Don't Fence Me In". Volunteer with

organizations that build and maintain trails and advocate for equestrian use or otherwise work to preserve our natural spaces.

Volunteering also builds valuable ties to land managers and with other trail user groups. Every user group has a stake in trails. It benefits all of us, in the long run, to get along and share these resources.

Being a trail rider involves understanding how to be a responsible steward and courteous to everyone enjoying the trails. Keep your horse trails open far into the future by being a good example of environmentally sound and socially responsible trail use.

See also Etiquette, Low Impact

A Trail Symphony

I had an opportunity to assist Ed, a longtime volunteer packer for the Olympic National Park, where he provides sturdy and reliable mule power to haul in the gear, food, and supplies required to keep the Park's backcountry functioning.

The project at hand was rebuilding the historic Bear Camp Shelter located deep within the Wilderness interior. We were tasked with transporting the equipment and food required to keep a party of backcountry carpenters supplied for eight days while they repaired and restored the aging structure.

The trip started in inky blackness at 4:00 am to arrive at the trailhead with time to saddle and ready the mules before the appearance of the work party. Park employees were delighted to find us waiting for them and able to accommodate the extra few comfort items that each had brought for their week plus stay in the backcountry. After carefully loading, weighing, and securing the gear, we embarked on the trek to our destination, nearly twenty miles and six hours away.

Blue sky was scarce as we made our way through the densely forested valley of the Dosewallips River. Along much of the route the trail meandered across gently rolling fields of emerald mosses punctuated periodically by broad tree trunks supporting the thick canopy casting a deep shade on the ground underneath.

As we made our way up the deep Dosewallips Valley, the trip became a musical event with the sounds of the pack string swirling through the air. Indeed, to think of this as a trail symphony wouldn't be out of place.

The rhythmic beat of hooves forms the percussion section, keeping a constant tempo as we head down the trail. The brass section is, of course, our bear bells. The steady ringing provides the melody of the trip; cowbells with their flat notes for cadence, Swiss bells with their higher-pitched harmonies, and the lone horse's sleigh bell providing musical punctuation for the tune. The symphony isn't just a percussion piece. The trees and the wind combine to form the woodwind section bringing resonance into the music with the wind softly rustling the leaves and limbs overhead. The continuous rushing of the river provides a soundscape as its waters inexorably seek their way to the ocean far away. The frequent water crossings bring periodic crescendos that slowly die away as we travel further down the trail to gradually rebuild as we near the next tributary.

The symphony ended as the evening's lengthening shadows welcomed us into our base camp destination. The process of unloading was commenced by the light of headlamps, followed by unsaddling and caring for the hungry *animals, and only then sharing a meal around the flickering light of the campfire. Needless to say, after a long day, there was no late-night revelry, and soon the sounds of mules on the highline permeated camp. My last recollection of the day was a brief glimpse of a meteor shooting across a small window in the forest canopy high above.*

Our trip was a success for everyone involved; we continued our volunteer efforts and improved the Olympic National Park with an uneventful pack trip, the Park had the Bear Camp Shelter improved, the backcountry carpenters didn't have to carry nearly 1,000 pounds of equipment on their backs, and we attended a noteworthy trail symphony.

RIDER

A rider actively influences their mount at all times. A rider is an

effective leader and makes the horse's job easier by using clear aids and a balanced seat. Riders are alert to their surroundings and are often able to stave off trouble before any outward signs are visible. A rider is what we should all aspire to be.

RIDING PARTNER

My best riding partner also happens to be my bride. Celeste doesn't like it when I ride alone if we can't hit the trails together. In the interest of family harmony, it's sometimes best to do what is asked of me. Generally, it's not too hard to find someone willing to go on a horse ride.

The hard part is finding the RIGHT someone to ride with.

Finding the right companion goes far beyond having a furry backyard beast and a few spare hours. I'll be the first to admit that I'm a self-centered kind of guy. I want to do everything that I can to ensure that I'll make it home in time for dinner. What follows is my list of interview questions to ask of any potential riding partner.

First Aid Certification? My life is important to me. If a ride moves past memorable and becomes eventful, I would like to know that whomever I'm riding with is able to help if I'm hurt. I ask to see the card because, unfortunately, everyone thinks they're knowledgeable. Sadly, being up to date with the latest ER episodes isn't the knowledge that I'm seeking. Please learn how to provide immediate care in emergencies. Please. You and I may never meet, but someone in your family or a random stranger may one day desperately need your help. Be able to provide it.

Medical Issues / Allergies? Bees and I are not friends, and I want all of my riding partners to know that and in which of my pockets the EpiPen lives. Some of my riding partners have cardiac issues. I want to know about those issues and where they keep their tiny vial of nitro-glycerine pills.

How Fast? Some people like to ride fast. Others like a slow steady walk. Both are valid options. Make sure that both parties enjoy the same thing. There's nothing more annoying than wanting to step out and being held back by a laggard or wishing to enjoy the scenery and being constantly prodded to move faster.

How Long? Agree on how long you want to ride before you set out. Some riders think 45 minutes makes for a fine trail ride. I like to spend a few hours in the saddle to justify the hassle of hooking up the trailer. Make sure that everyone is happy with the decision.

Where to Ride? Some riders aren't fond of hills; others find water crossings more hassle than they want. Take the time to discuss where you want to go to find the perfect area for both of your needs.

What's Your Animal Like? I'm not a fan of using the trails as a primary training area and so may be dis-inclined towards going out with a green beast that hasn't mastered the basics of Whoa, Go, and Steering at all gaits. Use your best judgment about what equine emotions you choose to be around. Nervous, high-strung animals tend to bring out the worst in my big red mule, while my wife's bay mare takes it all in stride.

Where to find the mythical unicorn who fits all your ride buddy criteria? With over 10 million owners of equines in the U.S., you're bound to find the perfect match if you look in the right places. Thankfully there are many opportunities for most of us to connect with a compatible trail partner. Many equine trail organizations and clubs offer activities and events where you can meet like-minded people. Participating in the work parties and pleasure rides hosted by these groups has resulted in long-lasting friendships.

PRO TIP

Make sure your prospective companion's answers match your ideas when it comes to an enjoyable trail ride.

Here are some of the best spots to find a potential trail ride partner.

Riding Clubs – There are many equine communities where you can meet other riders. These groups range from breed-specific organizations to trail advocacy associations, state horse councils, and social clubs. Most organizations have regular meetings where you'll get to know your horsey (muley?) neighbors. At the meetings, you'll find when and where various activities are taking place, including group trail rides. Start participating in the group's events, and in the process, you'll make friends with people who are probably just like you — looking for a riding partner.

Before you sign up for any group ride, be sure to ask questions to determine if the ride is suited to you and your animal's abilities. Find out how long the ride will be, the type of terrain, and the pace of the ride. If you aren't comfortable with the pace, distance, or terrain, keep searching for a club that is more in line with what you are seeking.

Prize Rides – A very popular type of group ride is the Prize or Poker ride. Many of these events are held every year to raise funds for clubs or charities.

Prize rides are a fun way to meet other trail riders and to enjoy an outing on the trail for a good cause. Socializing is often the biggest part of the rides, and it's hard to leave without having made a friend or two along the way.

Trail Competitions – Competitive trail events are a widespread and growing phenomenon across the U.S. Depending on how competitive you are and how much time and energy you want to invest in an event, you can choose from many different competitive trail activities.

There you have it, my take on what to look for in a riding partner and where to find a trail buddy. For me, trail riding is the most enjoyable of all equine activities. Riding with friends makes it even more extraordinary.

ROPE

To most people, a rope is a rope. They think there's no distinction  between polypropylene, manila, or how it's made, and that's a shame because materials and manufacturing methods offer different benefits in various situations. What works best as a climbing rope may be entirely inappropriate for rigging a highline. Here are a few points to consider when choosing ropes.

Material - Before synthetic rope came into being, people used natural materials for rope making. Now, most ropes are made of synthetic fibers like nylon and polypropylene. It is extremely important to know what materials and construction of rope you are using for each purpose. Some key things to look for when deciding what rope to use; include how strong and durable the material is and how much it stretches when in use or when wet.

Types of Rope

Nylon – Cheap, strong, and light. Sounds great until you factor in how quickly it degrades in the sun. It also stretches considerably when wet. This makes it a poor choice for highlines or other applications where you need a rope that doesn't change dimensions.

Polypropylene – Inexpensive, strong, and doesn't stretch. This is my go-to rope material.

Manila and Hemp – Natural fiber ropes have gone the route of the dinosaurs. Their lack of strength, excessive weight, and propensity to rot make these materials unsuited for modern camping.

Diameter vs. Strength – Modern synthetic ropes are very strong. Even very small diameter lines most likely have a higher breaking strength than you'll ever need. That being said, larger diameter ropes are easier to tie and much less likely to tangle than smaller diameter lines. My go-to rope diameter for packing purposes and general use around the farm is 3/8-inch. I've found that 1/8-inch diameter cord works well for camp utility work.

Rope Construction - There are also the options of having a braided or twisted rope. Braided rope is easy on the hands, has a core with a braided outer cover making it more flexible and resistant to kinking. Braided ropes are generally stronger than twisted. Twisted ropes may be more durable and easier to handle. Twisted ropes are also easier to splice than braided.

Ropes are part and parcel of horses and camping. Find a type that works well for you. We tend to use 3/8-inch polyester with three twisted strands for most of our camping and packing needs.

RULES AND REGS
Beyond the various generally accepted etiquette guidelines, knowing an area's rules and regulations before a trip can make your adventures go much smoother. The bare minimum information that I make the time to learn about, before a trip includes:

- Fire bans.
- Permits required.
- Weed Free Feed requirements.
- Bear restrictions.
- Equine Travel papers - Coggins, brand inspections, health certificates.

ABCs of Horse Camping

S

SADDLES

Saddle fit is all-important for trail horses. Properly fitting saddles help your horse stay sound, comfortable, and can even improve your comfort during long days on the trail.

Here are eight saddle tips to improve your trail rides.

Fit is everything – How your saddle fits your horse is the key to his comfort and soundness. The bars should lie parallel with the back muscles without touching the spine itself. The saddle's front arch should leave his withers free. It should also be wide and angled enough so that his shoulders are able to move freely. Find a reputable saddle maker and be leery of any overhyped claims. Keep in mind that a saddle that was perfect last year might not be perfect now. Horses change shape for any number of reasons, including weight gain, muscle gain, or simply due to aging.

Go light - Tired of slinging a 50-pound saddle? Consider investing in a lightweight trail saddle. Both you and your trail animal will appreciate the reduced pounds.

Use the right cinch - If your saddle doesn't fit, a cinch won't make it better. Overtightening the front cinch will only make your horse uncomfortable. Choose a cinch that's easy to clean, won't pick up trail debris, and won't rub or pinch your horse. Mohair cinches are excellent. Avoid fleece which is a magnet for debris.

Use a rear cinch - Consider a rear cinch. If your saddle is rigged to accommodate a flank cinch, use it. Be sure to use a hobble strap to keep the rear from becoming a bucking cinch.

Use a breast collar - A breast collar will help prevent your saddle from sliding toward your horse's rump. Select a wide, flat breast collar made from heavy leather or neoprene. Avoid any made from or covered in fleece.

Use a britchen or a crupper - Either will help prevent the saddle from sliding forward while going downhill. A britchen distributes pressure much better than a crupper which translates into a more comfortable time for your horse.

Don't fight the stirrup - If your saddle has stirrups whose natural position is sideways, you'll be plagued with sore ankles and knees. You can twist the fenders by soaking with water then twisting into the desired position. Put a broomstick through the stirrups to hold the fenders in position until they dry.

Use broad and deep stirrups - Broad and deep stirrups will give you maximum support over the ball of your foot when you're riding all day. Consider investing in shock-absorbing pads, which may improve foot and ankle comfort. Be careful with foam pads, as they tend to grip the soles of your boots.

SATELLITE MESSENGERS

Much like Personal Locator Beacons (PLBs), Satellite Messengers (SMs) are handheld transmitting devices useful in any area without reliable cell phone coverage. These user-friendly devices allow you to report on the status of your trip via text messages and your location coordinates to friends or family at home. They can also send a call for help in an emergency.

Unlike the phone you use every day, Satellite Messengers don't need a cellular signal to work. Instead, they use orbiting networks of satellites circling overhead. Not only are they used to track your position, but we can also use them to send and receive packages of data. We're talking around 140 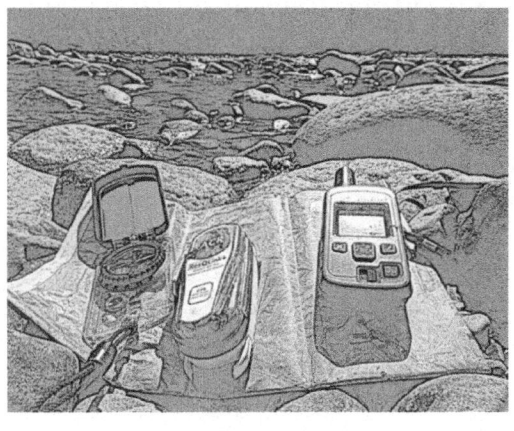 characters, similar to the early days of text messaging. That may not sound like much, but it's enough to tell your loved ones where you are (or that you're delayed), receive medical advice, and even download an up-to-date weather report.

Satellite Messengers are much less powerful than a PLB. A SPOT device only has 0.5 watts of power, where a PLB sends a signal that is ten times as powerful (5.0 watts) to push the message through trees, clouds, and anything else that could weaken the signal. A ten-fold difference is significant.

Satellite Messengers are GPS-based devices that rely on commercial satellite networks — generally, Iridium or Globalstar — rather than the military network used by PLBs. Emergency calls using either SMs network are routed to privately run coordination centers which then notify local 911 with your GPS location information.

Satellite Messenger devices usually cost less upfront than a PLB. However, these tools will not work without a paid subscription service. Each manufacturer offers a variety of usage plan options that may, in the long term, significantly increase your total cost for the unit. Unit prices range from under $100 to over $400. The subscription plans that are required to use the units vary widely depending on what features you want.

Three of the most promising Satellite Messengers are from SatPaq, SPOT, and Garmin. I won't sugarcoat it: None of these tools are perfect. Despite that, any of them could save your life when the trail gets rocky.

Each of these devices have a number of basic functions in common. When activated, all of them perform the following functions:
- In case of a non-life-threatening emergency, alert your personal contacts that you need help.

- In case of a life-threatening emergency, activate an SOS button that directly notifies emergency responders of your distress signal, as well as your GPS coordinates.
- Send text-based messages to your personal contacts.
- Create shareable online maps of your adventure so others can follow along in (near) real-time.
- Track your journey.

SatPaq

A clip-on antenna that turns your smartphone into a satellite communicator.

PRO: Inexpensive to purchase and to use. Takes advantage of the phone that's already in your pocket. CON: Requires an operable smart phone.

NIFTY FACT: The SatPaq communicates through Geostationary (GEO) satellites. GEO satellites don't move relative to your position on earth so they're always in view and your communications happen immediately without the delay that most other devices have.

Horse and mule riders like to get off the beaten path – We long for the backwoods and backcountry refuges of isolation where (hopefully) you won't see people for days. The problem when you're this far in the backcountry is that you're also well out of cell coverage. A lack of communication could make a bad situation much worse if there's a serious injury or illness. You won't have to worry about that potential worst-case scenario if you're carrying a SatPaq.

The SatPaq from Higher Ground is a lightweight device that easily clips to your smartphone and connects wirelessly using Bluetooth to communicate through satellites when there is no cell coverage. SatPaq's SpaceLinq free app allows you to send and receive messages, get instant weather forecasts, share your location, and get help in emergencies – all without having to pay monthly service fees. Users pay per message.

SatPaq also features an Artificial Intelligence medical service to answer first aid questions and an SOS service for emergencies. It's iPhone and Android compatible and will hold a charge for 4-5 months in storage. SatPaq only weighs 4 ounces — that's less than my iPhone!

SatPaq eliminates the monthly fees associated with other satellite messengers through the purchase of message credits called MessagePaqs that allow you to use the service whenever you need. These message credits holdover until you use them.

If you spend time exploring away from cell phone coverage, the SatPaq is a very attractive piece of gear.

SPOT X

A rugged communications device that will send texts independently, without a linked smartphone.

PRO: QWERTY keyboard and a built-in digital compass.

CON: Keyboard has tiny hard to use buttons. Cannot pair with a phone. Does not support maps.

The SPOT X is a stand-alone two-way satellite messaging device. The other devices we tested allow for two-way, customized messaging, but they require a smartphone for easy typing. The SPOT's built-in QWERTY keyboard makes it stand out. You compromise nothing by using the X on its own.

The Spot X sends and receives text messages and short emails. It is fundamentally different from SPOTS' other devices, such as the Gen3, which only send messages. Messages can be predefined, custom, or even posted to social media to keep all of your peeps in the know. Each Spot X unit is assigned a personal U.S. mobile  number, making sending messages to the device easy. The process of sending messages to the other devices we tested is less straightforward.

The battery life of the SPOT X far surpasses that of the Garmin inReach; going twice as long (10 days) before a recharge is required.

Along with sending and receiving messages, the SPOT X is also able to track your location at regular intervals; send SOS messages directly to the GEOS International Emergency Response Coordination Center; and function as a rudimentary navigation device with a built-in compass and the ability to set waypoints.

The SPOT X is a solid backcountry communications option, so long as you can accept the keyboard and lack of mapping capabilities.

Garmin inReach

Garmin inReach devices use the iridium satellite network of 66 low orbit satellites offering 100% coverage worldwide to help ensure your messages are received.

SM devices allow users to communicate via text message to friends, family, and rescue operators at a fraction of the price of regular satellite phones. These tools also allow for continuous tracking so that contacts back home can follow along with your journey.

PRO: Reliable, Rugged, Accurate, Preloaded topographic maps.
CON: Unit is bulky, heavy, expensive.

Both versions of the inReach excel at messaging, as long as you set your expectations appropriately. Satellite communications, no matter the network or the technology employed, have inherent limitations. Sometimes you'll have to wait a few minutes for satellites to pass overhead and send and receive the messages. The simplest way to send messages with the inReach is through the Garmin EarthMate smartphone app. On the app, it's easy to add your contacts and then send and receive a big batch of messages. Pre-programmed messages make it much easier to send quick updates, so you don't have to type the same message multiple times. Without the phone app, composing messages is a painfully slow process of ticking off characters on the inReach keypad.

Which Satellite Messenger Should YOU Pick?

Your answer will depend on your unique needs. Here are the main questions that I consider before choosing a device.

- What are your biggest priorities? Easy, quick messaging? Battery life? Cost savings? Compact size and weight? Navigational tools?
- Do you plan to also carry a smartphone and use it in conjunction with your satellite messenger, or do you want a standalone device?

Beyond the classic 10 essentials, modern SM devices provide a greater increase in your overall outdoor safety than most other gear available. They offer peace of mind for your loved ones and two-way communication with search and rescue teams and medical professionals. Simply put, you should buy one, learn to use it, show your riding partners how to operate the device, and bring it with you on every ride.

See also Communications, Personal Locator Beacons

SAWS ON THE TRAIL

Trees happen, and they occasionally fall. It's better to have a saw than to turn around.

Sometimes you can simply step over or ride around fallen limbs and downed trunks. Just as often, it's not safe to do so. Additionally, riding around a barrier instead of removing it leads to multiple user paths

weaving through an area, causing further erosion, mud, and other issues. It's better to clear the trail. After all you wanted to stretch, and your horse wants a quick break too. Clearing trails is a good practice to foster. You're helping your fellow trail users and land managers, as well as promoting riders as responsible trail users.

What Type of Saw?

There are many types of saws readily available. We're going to stick with the following manual types. Pocket chainsaws, Fixed, and Folding blades.

Pocket Chainsaw

These handy survival tools consist of chainsaw blades with handles at both ends that allow the operator to cut through smaller branches. Unlike their much heavier cousins with motors, a pocket chainsaw weighs less than a pound and is easily carried in your saddlebags.

Fixed Blade Saw

Fixed blade, or rigid handle, saws are heavier and slightly harder to pack than the types previously mentioned. But they work better and are much sturdier. Cutting lumber is work; why make it any harder? A fixed blade saw in a sturdy sheath will ride nearly unnoticed under your riding saddle's fenders.

Folding Saw

Folding saws are designed to give you the cutting ability of a fixed blade saw but in a compact and lightweight design that is safe to carry in your saddle bags. Blades of these saws are safely out of harm's way once folded into the built-in sheath.

How Big?

Size matters. Yes, it does. The maximum cut you can make with a saw depends on the length of the blade. For an efficient cutting action, you want plenty of travel on each stroke. In theory, an 18" blade will get through a 17" log but you'll be making plenty of tiny push-pull movements and it's going to take forever. As a guide, if you're looking to cut up to 6" logs then a blade of 10" to 12" is fine.

For most of us, the choice between a pocket chainsaw, folding saw, or fixed blade will come down to how often you're going to use it. Do you want a "just in case" saw, or do you want to be prepared for whatever nature throws at you?

I don't know about in your part of the world, but in the Pacific Northwest, riders always find blowdown across the trail, and the next time the wind blows, there will be even more. I don't leave the trailhead without a sturdy fixed blade saw.  Often, it's "Little Joe" a 20" saddle saw. If I'm going on a pack trip, "Stella" my 40" crosscut will ride under my pack saddle boxes.

ABCs of Horse Camping

What To Look For:

Whichever type of saw you choose here are a few considerations worth noting:

- Sharpness – It doesn't matter how good the rest of the saw is, if the blade isn't sharp, you're going to have a tough time. The best blades not only start sharp but are tempered and coated so they stay sharp.
- Cutting Efficiency – How much wood is removed with each stroke? Cutting efficiency depends on a combination of elements such as blade length, sharpness, and cutting teeth design. Some blades only cut on the pull stroke while others cut on both.
- Handle - You want an ergonomic handle design that sits comfortably in the hand, including when you are wearing gloves.
- Safety – Sharp saw blades will cut more than just wood. Make sure you have a way of keeping the blade safe so it only cuts when you want it to.
- Lightweight – You want your saw to be easy to carry but reduced weight sometimes means reduced overall structural integrity. Saws with shorter blades and polymer, rather than metal, handles, and frames may save you a few ounces.
- Sharpening / Replacing Blades – Make sure that the saw you buy can be sharpened or uses a blade that is easily replaced. The cost of some replacement blades sometimes gets close to the cost of a new saw.

Not all saws are created equal, so it pays to spend a little extra to buy a well-made product. The best saw, regardless of type, will have a sharp, quality blade.

Look for design elements that will improve the efficiency of your cutting strokes, so you go through more wood with less work. Weight is always a concern but don't be too quick to discount the benefits of carrying a saw.

Some type of saw is a must-have for every serious trail rider. I carry one and just about everyone that I know does so as well. At some point you're going to encounter a log, a blowdown, or a tree with branches pointing in every direction that you cannot easily go over or around. By carrying a saw you'll be able to clear the path and be back on your way in short order.

Before you start making sawdust take a few minutes to learn how to do so safely. Certified sawyer classes are widely available through many trail organizations and will take your wood cutting efforts to the next level.

SHELTER

Searching for the perfect camping shelter is similar to looking for a new house. The options are virtually endless, with myriads of styles, sizes, materials, and features to consider. Here's how to pick the right one for every adventure.

Over the past decade, I've spent an average of about 30 days in backcountry Wilderness areas each year. Each of those nights found me in some type of shelter out of the worst of the weather.

How big? Size matters. Taking more shelter than you need adds unnecessary cargo weight and volume for your riding or pack animals to carry. Finding the "goldilocks zone" of just enough space without going overboard is key. When I first started venturing into backcountry areas, I had only my riding animals to carry camp, so weight and volume were huge factors that led me to tarps, bivy sacks, hammocks, and small tents. Now that I have pack animals, I can live a bit better.

Tarps

To me, tarps are the MacGyver of backcountry shelters and on par with duct tape in terms of versatility. They're ultralight and take up little space. While you can use the blue tarps from your local hardware store, tarps designed for camping are made of lightweight, high-tech materials that are both waterproof and tear resistant.

Bivy Sacks and Shelters

Think of these as a waterproof slipcover for your sleeping bag. They're a bit spartan but sleeping under the stars while still being protected from the bugs and rain is a wonderful feature. If a bivy is too bare-bones, a similar type of shelter is a hybrid of a bivy and traditional tent. I think of my bivy shelter as a low-rise tent that covers the upper half of my body. This gain in space adds a couple of pounds to the weight but provides a comfort zone that allows for better ventilation than a bivy sack.

Tents

Tents are tricky because there are so many types and styles on the market. Short ones, tall ones, ultra-light to quite heavy. High-tech and low-tech. Deciding which one is right for you can be interesting.

241

The factors I consider before I buy a new tent.

How am I going to use it?

Be honest. Will it be for campground camping? Or do you need to haul it deep into the backcountry? If you'll only use it while trailhead or campground camping, weight shouldn't be a significant concern. On the other hand, anytime you ask your horse to carry your home on his back, it's only fair to go as light as possible.

How many people will it house?

Tent interiors are built snug to save on material. Snug as in cramped. I like a little more space, so my rule of thumb is to look for a size that's one person larger than the number of people going. Just you and the spouse? Get a three-person tent. Is the dog coming too? Get a 4-person tent. With this rule, you'll have plenty of space and minor weight penalty. More room means more comfort.

How much does it weigh?

Everyone wants a camping tent that is light, spacious, and durable. The challenges for both consumers and manufacturers are that weight, space, and materials fight against each other. In many ways, weight boils down to ounces carried vs. dollars spent. Some materials are ultra-lightweight and boast astronomical price tags. On the other hand, a cheap tent may be inexpensive but weigh significantly more. The correlation between space and weight is easy. More area equals more fabric, therefore, more weight.

What materials?

Choosing materials is more of a challenge. The material that a tent is made from will dramatically affect weight, price, and durability. The main question here is nylon vs. polyester. Nylon is stronger, lighter, and more packable than polyester. Polyester is cheaper than nylon. I stick with ripstop nylon for my tents. It may cost a little more, but the longer life of nylon helps reduce the lifetime cost.

How tall?

Comfort is important. I used to crawl into my tent at the end of the day and think nothing of it. Those days are gone. Now, one of the most important features is being able to stand upright in my tent. Backcountry trips should be for building beautiful memories, not "character building" expeditions.

If you've spent time in smaller, backpacking tents, the ability to stand up and move freely around your tent upright is an eye-opener. I've enjoyed the palatial spaciousness of canvas wall tents, but their extreme weight and bulk have kept me from taking the plunge. I don't have enough pack animals for this kind of luxury. Enter pyramid-style tents with their tall centers that allow you to walk, not crawl, through the door.

SNACKING ON THE TRAIL

A great trail ride on a fall day, heading out from the trailhead, letting the sun warm you, and enjoying a terrific ride; what a day! Until your horse decides he's hungry on a sketchy bit of trail, and you lose count of how many times he's yanked the reins from your hands in an unending tug of war.

I've been there, as have many other riders. At best, it's a hassle, and at worst downright dangerous. I used to allow the equine I belonged to, LT, to grab a bite whenever he wanted. After all, he was working hard to haul me around; why not let him grab a quick snack? Things changed when I started riding on the sides of mountains in the Cascade Range, where it was vitally important for LT to pay more attention to where he was placing his feet than on that tempting sprig of grass just off the trail.

Clearly, our expectations were diverging on the topic of appropriate times and places to eat. I'm sure that many of us have faced similar situations.

Correcting this disconnect between your expectations and the reality of the situation requires us to consider what kind of training, if any, that we've done with our mount.

What kind of trail riding education has your horse gone through? Is your animal a distinguished graduate student of the trail riding academy, or is he a remedial student? Horses go through rigorous training programs for arena jobs, but often we expect our mounts to just "know" how to handle the trail.

We get frustrated and upset when they don't perform flawlessly because we don't understand that horses and mules need to be taught trail riding just as they're taught any other equine activity, from roping and eventing to dressage and beyond. There are many good reasons why experienced riders start with groundwork and then introduce a new animal to the trail ponied to a veteran horse or mule. Only after many hours and miles of school will the new kid graduate to a full-fledged trail animal ready to take a rider safely into the backcountry and back.

When we train for the rigors of the trail, we battle against the equine's prevailing nature that helps horses avoid danger and preserve their status within the herd. While we may not be able to eliminate these innate behaviors completely, we aim to teach our mounts to endure the unnatural events that they'll encounter, to listen to our requests, and to relax and enjoy the job of traveling down the trail safely and efficiently.

For many horses, grazing is to them what chocolate is to us; irresistible. You really can't blame them. Equines are grazing animals designed to eat small amounts of grass continually. However, this rationale doesn't make your trail ride any more pleasant as the reins are pulled from your grasp time and time again. So, the objective becomes how to arrive at a working compromise between the human and the horse, so each of us achieves our goals.

For any compromise to work, we have to be reasonable. Equines love fresh grass; after all, it is their natural food. We should understand that grazing on the trail is a very natural urge for them to want to do. Trail snacking isn't rude or bad; it's their version of chocolate. I don't expect LT to understand that a saddle equals no food. If that were to happen, I doubt that he'd continue to run to the gate when I hook up the trailer. Instead, what we as trail riders can do is to teach our mounts a grazing cue that means "OK, here and now is a great place

ABCs of Horse Camping

to eat". For LT and me, that cue is lowering the reins and a pat on LT's neck.

Teaching LT that loose reins and a pat mean that it's ok to eat took a little while; after all, there's no free lunch. But it paid off in rides that became much more enjoyable and saved a lot of time, effort, and arguments along the way.

The steps I took in LT's grass-grabbing re-education included making the "right" choices easy for him. Don't stand your beast in the middle of a meadow and expect him not to want to taste that choice grass. Instead, start this training program where the graze is marginal at best and slowly work your way into more tempting locations.

LT's re-education also required me to concentrate on my level of awareness. How many people are riders, and how many are passengers? Just as our mounts need to be aware of their surroundings, so must we be mindful of our mount. A rider is aware of everything going on and is able to make changes or corrections before problems occur. A passenger is just cargo for the horse to pack. Don't be cargo; be attentive to your mount and what he's thinking and re-direct his thoughts before he dives after that equine version of trail chocolate.

See also Training

STOVES

A stove is one of the essential items you'll carry when camping because making tea and coffee, as well as cooking meals, are everyday rituals when you're in the wilderness. Let's go into what to consider and what to look for in camp stoves.

After a few decades of horse camping, I've managed to collect a few stoves. It's nice to be able to pick and choose, but at the end of the day, I generally only take one on a trip.

Choosing a stove may seem a bewildering challenge, given the number of options. That said, as with any piece of gear, the process of selecting the best stove for your needs becomes pretty straightforward if you hash out a few basic details.

The way I figure it there are only 4 types of stoves: Canister Stoves - Liquid Fuel Stoves - Alcohol Stoves – Wood Burning Stoves.

Canister Stoves

They're light, compact, easy to use, and fast. With canister stoves, there's no priming, pumping, or maintenance of any kind. Just screw in your fuel canister and light it up for a quick meal.

On the other hand, the fuel for canister stoves is expensive, they don't work well in the cold (usually below 20°F), they're prone to be tippy, and most canisters aren't reusable, making them an ecological nightmare.

Canister Stove Summary
PROS:

Light & compact - Rapid boil times.

Easy to use - Clean burn - no pot residue.

CONS:

More expensive fuel - Can be tippy.

Not as good as liquid fuel stoves in cold weather.

It may be hard to find a recycling center that accepts the empties.

In the past I used canister stoves but have since shifted to liquid fuel stoves, mostly because of their instability and difficulty in recycling.

Liquid Fuel Stoves

Liquid fuel stoves work well in below-freezing conditions, and their fuel (white gas) is much cheaper than canister stove fuel. Some liquid fuel stoves may be used with different fuel types (including kerosene, unleaded, and even diesel fuel). Most liquid fuel stoves offer stable bases and, of course, the more cost-effective fuel.

Liquid Fuel Stove Summary
PROS:

Fuel is less expensive - Good for extreme cold.

Fuel bottles are refillable & easier to gauge usage.
CONS:
Heavier & bulkier than some others – Tends to be noisy.
More complicated to use - priming required.

I think liquid fuel stoves are your best bet if you're planning to do a lot of cooking, and I am. From my ancient Coleman two-burner to newer high-tech models, white gas stoves have a place in my kit.

Alcohol Stoves

Alcohol stoves are light, silent, simple to use, and denatured alcohol is easy to find.

The main downsides with alcohol stoves are the slow cook times, poor performance in the cold, and less efficient fuel.

Cooking times for alcohol stoves can be decreased with a system like this Trangia setup which helps block the wind and holds heat against your pots to increase efficiency. But even with a good windscreen, cooking with an alcohol stove will require more patience.

Be careful when using alcohol stoves because their fuel burns with a clear blue flame that is very hard to see. Always make sure your stove has entirely burned out before handling it or attempting to refuel. Additionally, most alcohol stoves aren't permitted for use during fire bans.

Alcohol Stove Summary
PROS:
    Light & compact – Inexpensive.
    Easy to make your own.
    Easy to find fuel - Very quiet.
CONS:
    Slow cooking times - Less efficient fuel.
    Poor performance in wind - Poor temperature control.
    Hard to see the flame, easy to spill fuel.
    Can't use during most fire bans.

Wood Burning Stoves

Wood stoves are a popular option among people that like doing

things the old-fashioned way. Using a wood stove is very similar to cooking over a campfire but quicker and more efficient.

With a wood stove, you won't have to carry any fuel, you'll be able to cook longer, you'll be burning a renewable resource, and you'll get to enjoy the comforts of a warm fire nearly every night.

Wood stoves do have some significant downsides. They require more time and effort than most backpacking stoves, which is frustrating when you're tired and hungry after a long day of riding. It may also be tough to find good fuel in rainy weather.

Lastly, wood stoves are illegal to use during most fire bans.

Wood Stove Summary
PROS:
  Minimal fuel weight - Minimal fuel cost.
  Renewable fuel resource - Nostalgic & pleasant.
CONS:
  More time, effort & practice are required.
  Slower cook times - Usually heavier.
  Can't use during most fire bans.

I hope that this helps you to choose a camp stove that works best for your style of camping.

SWIVEL
The connection point between critter and highline involves an anchor point to attach our pony's leads. There are many gadgets for this application, from Patent-pending thingamajigs, rings, and all sorts of superfluous junk that does one thing only. My feeling is that uni-taskers are the antithesis of camping and have no place in my gear bag.

For years, my highline connection point has been a length of climbing cord fashioned into a prusik that freely twists and untwists. For decades, I've said that if my animals can turn left while on a highline, they are also able to turn to the right. By golly, that was true for many years, on more camping trips than I remember and, well, you get the idea. My no-swivel system worked great. Until it didn't.

My main riding mule, Ruger, had several very long, very uncomfortable nights during a pack trip into the Eagle Cap Wilderness. Every night of the trip he twisted his lead into knots. Each morning I would find Ruger, his head lifted high, standing patiently, waiting for me to untie his halter and release him from his prison. I will add that on the same trip my go-to pack mule, Ellie never had an issue and would watch Ruger's plight with equine amusement. I think Ellie double-dog-dared Ruger to repeatedly turn in the same direction – Mules do have a sense of humor.

It could have been much worse, and I regret that I ever let such a thing happen. He'd never had an issue before. I guess Ruger just decided that turning left was tedious after walking in clockwise circles. I failed Ruger in acknowledging that an issue could occur but neglecting to proactively remedy that potential situation. Sorry, Ruger.

Enter the swivel. No, not the cheap barrel swivels found in most uni-taskers. I wanted something stronger and more reliable. I went swivel searching to find something that would be strong, reliable, small, and lightweight. The worlds of rock climbing and commercial arborists were most helpful.

There are two main types of swivels: barrel and ball bearing.

- Barrel swivels have a middle barrel that has been loosely wrapped, or swaged, with another piece of metal that rotates around the barrel. The best part of these is the price. They're cheap to make and to buy. The bad thing is that the metal-on-metal grinding creates friction that over time will result in problems, including premature wear and breakage.
- Ball bearing swivels on the other hand contain polished stainless-steel ball bearings positioned between the spindle and body. This enables the swivel to rotate freely, negating any twist, even under heavy load. The perceived disadvantage of ball-bearing swivels is their price. However, in certain situations — such as when our ponies are involved — you can't afford not to use them.

The comfort of Ruger and the girls is important to me, so I went with climbing grade ball bearing swivels. These brightly colored beauties weigh little, spin like butter, and are significantly stronger (with a rating of 35kN, nearly 8,000 pounds) than other well-marketed inline swivels.

I haven't had any issues with anyone getting twisted up after adding a ball-bearing swivel to each prusik loop that I anchor the bubbas to on the highline. A simple swivel makes for a better night's rest for my mules and me. It should go without saying that better nights make for better trips.

See also Highline, Prusik

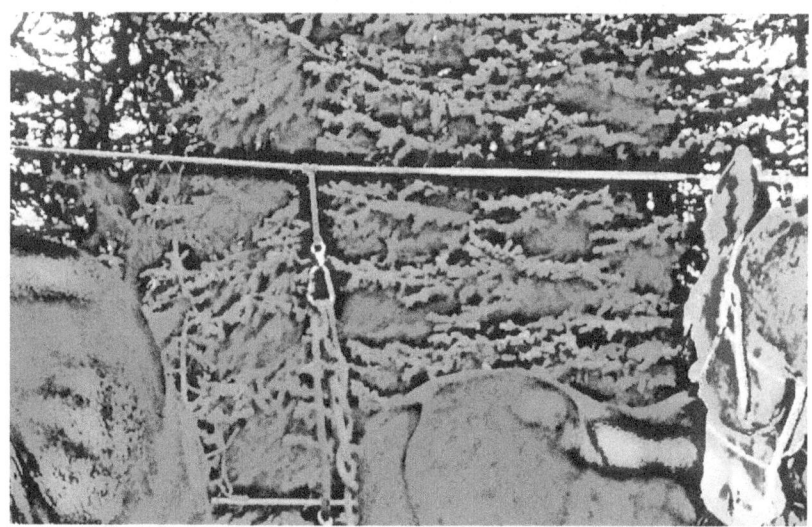

ABCs of Horse Camping

T

TERRAIN ASSOCIATION

Terrain association is the comparison of the landscape you see with your eyes in the real world vs. the terrain depicted on a topo map. You're looking for more than the roads and exits that you would find in a road atlas. Instead, it's the terrain features such as hills, ridges, rivers, etc. You can use terrain association to confirm your location by looking around and identifying terrain features around you and then matching those features with their corresponding contour lines on the map.

See also Contour Lines, Maps

TRAILER

Having horses keeps us on the move and not just heading down the trail. Even if we're fortunate enough to have a local trail system handy, we'll soon want to travel further afield to enjoy new trails and new adventures. This requires us to have a way to haul our animals safely and efficiently from point A to where we want to be.

Let's talk about the essentials to look for in any horse trailer. Use this list of features the next time you're shopping for a new or used trailer to ensure that both you and your horses are safe and comfortable.

PRO TIP

Speaking of trailer value: Don't let "used" scare you. Often a good used trailer is a much better value than a cheap new trailer. A well-maintained high-quality trailer will hold not only its value much longer but could also be safer. Cheap sometimes equals poorly made and unsafe.

Here are ten factors to consider when you're hunting for a trailer.

Ramp or step? – How your horse enters the trailer is a concern, and each option has its own set of pros and cons. Ramps must be low, sturdy, and provide good traction. If a step is your choice, be sure that the rear edge of the trailer is padded or at least rounded to help prevent any injury if the horse should slip off. Just as some horses may take offense to the hollow sound of hooves walking up a ramp, some are uncomfortable with the big step up or out of a step-up trailer. I prefer a step-up trailer but try to expose my animals to ramps as often as possible, just in case.

Straight, Stock or Slant? – I think if a horse got to pick, it would pick a roomy stock trailer over anything else. The second choice would be a slant load and the third a straight load trailer. Slant load trailers offer more efficient use of space, and often a slant is shorter (and easier to maneuver) than a straight load trailer of similar capacity.

Bigger is Better – Horses are large animals, and they need a big space to ride happily and safely in. When you're considering size, think in all three dimensions, length, height, and width of the horse's compartment. Width and length will let your horse use his legs to stay balanced and extra height will let him move his head as well as keep him much cooler by providing extra air space. A taller trailer may also look less like a cave and be more inviting for the horse.

Color Matters – As snazzy as they may look, dark-colored trailers will absorb heat just like the dark seats in your car and can make the trailer uncomfortably warm or even unsafely hot. Stick with a light color for your trailer to help keep everyone cool. The interior color is also important. Dark interior colors will make the trailer seem like a dark and hostile cave. Light and airy are the key feelings to look for. Stock trailers are wonderful in this regard, with lots of openings for light and air. Many "problem loaders" that balk at entering a standard trailer will walk right into a stock trailer.

Divided We Stand – Dividers are a source of division for many horse owners. Some are fond of partial dividers that let a horse spread his legs wider. Others favor full dividers that keep horses from stepping on each other's legs or slipping under a divider. Another faction advocates no dividers at all such as in a stock trailer.

Aluminum or Steel – Aluminum weighs less than steel and won't corrode as quickly. Steel is stronger than aluminum and offers some increased protection but also is prone to rust.

Flooring Material - The two primary materials here are wood  or aluminum, and each has its benefits. Wooden floors, most commonly found in steel trailers, have many benefits. They are strong, last for many years, allow for excellent drainage, and are far less expensive to install and replace than aluminum. Floors made of aluminum weigh less than wood, are very durable, and are extremely easy to clean. Regardless of flooring type, mats will keep your horses from slipping and ride more comfortably.

Drop-down or Sliding Windows – Drop-down windows provide a larger opening and more airflow to help keep the horse comfy. Sliders take up less room. Regardless of the type of window make sure to have bars to keep the horse's heads inside and screens to keep flying debris out. If you've ever had a bug hit you while driving you understand why both are good ideas.

Bumper Pull vs. Gooseneck – Your towing vehicle will be a significant influence on this factor. A gooseneck can't be towed by an SUV, but it provides excellent storage and sleeping areas. The gooseneck is also wonderful in terms of superior turning control and maneuverability. Bumper pull trailers are usually less expensive and require less space to store them when you're not on the road.

Suspension – No horse enjoys bumping and bouncing down the road. Help smooth the ride so that your animals are fresh and ready for the trail, not worn out from the ride there. Leaf springs ensure that the axle loads are always balanced, and they used to be the standard for trailer suspension. Rubber torsion axles are said to have a smoother ride than leaf spring suspensions. The downside to torsion axles is that they don't equalize or balance the load, which could put undue pressure on a single tire.

TRAILER MAINTENANCE

Now is a good time for your horse trailer's yearly safety checks and service. If you aren't mechanically savvy or just not inclined to do the job yourself, a qualified professional can do all the work for you. Just make sure that they know what you want examined as the mechanic may not be familiar enough with horse trailers unless you ask for specific tasks.

Easy Trailer Inspections To Do Yourself - and two that I leave for the pros!

Inspecting Your Trailer Tires

- Check the tire pressure

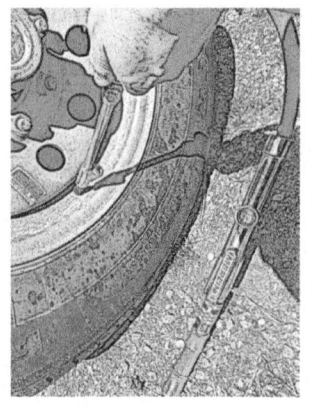

One of the most common issues drivers face with their trailer tires is under inflation. Under inflation of your tires causes your tires to wear more quickly and could even cause a blowout. Unfortunately, due to a trailer tire's stiff sidewalls, most won't bulge out when the pressure is low like a car tire. The only way to accurately check your PSI is with a quality pressure gauge.

To check the pressure in your tires, look for the PSI recommendation from the trailer manufacturer. The PSI should be listed in the owner's manual, or on a plaque on the trailer body. The tire inflation recommendation is according to the max load capacity of the trailer itself, not the amount written on the side of the tire. Check your tire pressure before each trip.

- Visually inspect the tread and sidewall

While you're checking your tire's air pressure, look for foreign objects that may be caught in the tread, cracking, or bulges on the sidewall that may indicate a broken cord. Tires that are overly worn or cracked can lead to potential blowouts, putting you and your loved ones at risk.

If you see cracks on the circumference of your trailer tires, be careful. This indicates dry rot, which makes tires more susceptible to problems. More horse trailer tires wear out from rot rather than from road miles. Trailer tires often sit for prolonged periods. This creates flat spots that are high-risk for separation. Additionally, UV light from the sun contributes to cracking and premature aging.

Finally, you want to ensure that there is a valve cap on every tire. These cost just a few dollars but protect the tire valve from damage.

- Measure the Tread Depth

Tread depth is the measurement from the top of the tread to the bottom of the tire's deepest grooves. It determines if the tire can maintain safe tracking and handling performance. An easy way to tell if the tires have neared the end of their life is by using a penny to confirm the tire's tread depth. If Lincoln's entire head is visible, then the tire is considered worn out in most instances and should be replaced.

- How old are my trailer tires?

All tires sold in the US have a DOT code that indicates the tire meets all federal standards; these identification numbers also include the tire's date of manufacture. It is recommended to replace trailer tires every 3-7 years. When purchasing new trailer tires, talk to the dealer to ensure the product that you are receiving has been recently manufactured.

To find your tire's date code, identify the code on the tire that begins with "DOT". A series of letters and numbers should follow the "DOT". The last four digits of this code tell you the date when your tire was manufactured. The first two numbers indicate what week of the year it was made, and the second two numbers represent the year. For example, 1203 would reveal that a tire was manufactured during the 12th week, or mid-March, of 2003.

By taking these easy steps, you can extend the life of your tires while decreasing your risk. Don't forget to check your spare tire.

Inspecting Your Trailer Floor

The trailer floor must be in good condition. Take out the mats and check the floor for soundness. Your horses are counting on it.

If you have a wood floor, test its integrity with a screwdriver or a knife. Try to stick a screwdriver into the surface and twist it. If the wood crumbles easily it's time to replace the floorboards. Do the same from underneath. Rot may be hiding where you can't easily see it.

If you have an aluminum floor, check for corrosion or pitting. Also, check the welds for cracks. If you see a potential problem, contact the dealer.

Inspecting Trailer Lights

Turn on the lights. Are all the taillights, brakelights, clearance lights, and turn signals working properly? Replace bulbs as necessary. Verify that the trailer's electrical connection to your vehicle is clean and tight.

Inspect Safety Chains

Trailer safety chains are the first line of defense in case anything causes a sudden disconnection of tow vehicle and trailer. If your ball or coupler does fail, your safety chains will allow you to guide your trailer and ease your way into a stop.

Check the chains for wear and tear. Replace as needed. Ensure that the chains are attached to the towing vehicle's frame, not to any part of the hitch. When connected, the chains should not drag on the ground or be twisted to shorten them.

Safety chains should never be overlooked for regular maintenance, they're the glue holding your towing adventure together.

Inspect the Breakaway Battery and Switch

The trailer breakaway system is designed to automatically bring the trailer to a safe stop should the trailer be disconnected from the tow vehicle while driving. For this to happen, you must have operational electric brakes on the trailer, the 12-volt battery must be charged, and the switch cable must be attached to the towing vehicle.

Ensure that the breakaway cable is NOT attached to the hitch or the safety chains. Doing so is neither legal nor safe. The breakaway cable should be attached to a part of the tow vehicle that cannot fall off, such as the frame.

A quick way to check if the breakaway system is working is as follows:

1) Hook up the trailer but keep the trailer's electrical plug disconnected.
2) Pull out the pin from the breakaway switch.
3) Slowly pull the tow vehicle forward. If the trailer brakes lock up & the wheels won't turn, your breakaway system is working.

If your trailer rolls without restraint, you need to have the system repaired. Re-insert the pin into the switch.

Inspect the Trailer Jack
Operate the jack to ensure that it raises and lowers the trailer smoothly when connecting and disconnecting from the tow vehicle.

Ensure the jack is stable and tightly fastened to the trailer. For swivel jacks, check mounting/swivel hardware for worn or broken parts. Grease if needed.

Inspect the Inside of the Trailer
Look inside the trailer for any potential problems. Do all moving parts, doors, and latches work properly? Ensure that no animals or insects have built unwelcome homes since the trailer was last used.

Trailer Inspections that I Delegate to a Professional

Wheel Bearings and Hubs
Trailer wheel bearings need regular maintenance, and with enough towing, replacement. The bearings are located within the wheel hub and reduce the friction between the wheel and wheel assembly. Because the bearings are hidden from plain view, it is crucial to

remember to take the necessary time to open the wheel hub and inspect.

Wheel hubs connect the trailer tires to the axle and allow them to spin. Check to see if they are damaged, corroded, or improperly installed to avoid issues such as impaired steering or a broken axle.

Brake Shoes and Drums

Properly functioning brake shoes and drums are essential to ensure your and your animals, safety. As such, they should be inspected for excessive wear or heavy scoring. Depending on the amount of wear, the drums may have to be turned or replaced.

Regular trailer maintenance is critical to ensuring the longevity of your trailer, as well as helping you arrive at your destination safely. If you have specific questions regarding your trailer, consult your owner's manual or your dealer.

TRAINING THE TRAIL HORSE AND THE TRAIL RIDER

I love Merriam-Webster's definition of training; "The process by which an athlete prepares for competition by exercising, practicing, etc.". We, and our mounts, are athletes, and trail riding is not an endeavor where we can expect success without preparation.

Trail riding is generally a wonderful experience. It can also be horrible, and we've all been there. In riding backcountry and front country areas across the US, I've watched and noted what differentiates the successful from the not-so-successful riders. I've found that the riders having the best time and the most fun are those who have prepared themselves and their mounts before arriving at the trailhead.

From what I've seen, the quickest way to shake a rider's confidence is the inability to ask the horse to perform a task without confusion or resistance. We as riders need to learn the cues to effectively communicate our requests without becoming unsure of ourselves. To help in the learning process, I've found that a good riding instructor, who has experience with trail riding, as opposed to show, or arena training, is invaluable.

Preparing for a successful trail ride goes beyond having a solid foundation in the basics of equine education. Before a horse and rider team arrive at the trailhead, the equine should be comfortable standing quietly, moving forward freely, and moving off the rider's leg. The rider should be able to use all of the basic riding aids, and the horse should be willing and able to respond appropriately.

Once you've mastered the basics, you'll be ready for the advanced schooling that will become important for trail riding. A few of the

ABCs of Horse Camping

secondary skills that you and your horse should possess include the following:

Neck Reining - The ability to steer with one hand is one of the most useful skills to master for trail riding. I see neck-reining as the ability to ride primarily with seat and leg cues; if your horse is light and willing to be guided off subtle aids, it's very easy to free up a hand for other jobs.

PRO TIP

Having a free hand allows the rider to move low hanging branches out of the way, grab a snack, or lead a pack string.

Backing - It only takes one trip down a narrow trail to appreciate a horse that will back willingly and allow itself to be steered backward to safety. The ability to back my horse out of a tight situation has been the escape path for my curiosity more than once. Practice backing on varied terrain and through obstacles to practice responsiveness and trust. Your horse should also be able to stop and wait quietly.

Leg Yields and Sidepassing - If you value your knees, you'll quickly appreciate the ability to ask your mount to move away from that very large, very hard tree. Sidepassing is only different in that the horse is standing still when you ask him to step to the side, perhaps for a hiker with a small child in tow. Most riders can move their horse sideways, but few do it precisely. Think of moving only one step, or a specific foot sideways.

Mounting from Both Sides – This is a very valuable skill to learn and practice. I'm not nearly tall enough to mount from the downhill side of many trails and in many areas turning around to mount from the "correct" side isn't feasible. Your horse should be able to stand quietly while you mount and get settled in the saddle, then wait for your cue to go.

De-Sensitizing - Expose your mount to as many of the sights he'll meet on the trail as possible. I'd much rather have my horses encounter bicycles at home for the first time rather than on the trail. While you'll never eliminate a spook, you'll be surprised at how much they can be reduced by constantly exposing your animals to new stimuli. I often ride my bike in the paddock with a backpack on. It looks silly, but LT now takes most encounters in stride. Be aware of potentially scary meetings; teach your horse to be curious and trust where you place his feet.

We live in an amazing place and exploring it on horseback can be phenomenal. A little bit of preparation will ensure that it is.

See also Confidence, Water Crossing Training

TREE SAVER STRAPS

Tree Saver Straps are simply a length of webbing that distributes the pressure of a highline to protect trees. Located under the bark is the living, working part of the tree. Compromise the protective bark layer, and you could harm or kill the tree. That's why responsible outdoors people use Tree Saver Straps to protect the trees.

See also Highline

PRO TIP

Tree Saver Straps made of brightly colored materials are less likely to be lost.

TRUCKER'S HITCH

A Trucker's Hitch is created from a series of knots forming a crude block and tackle that amplifies the force applied to a rope. Loops of rope are used instead of pulleys in this system which effectively doubles the user's strength and creates a tight highline that is, in turn, much safer, without resorting to gadgets.

Steps to Tying a Trucker's Hitch

1 - Tie one end of your rope to a tree saver strap. About 7-10 feet from the opposite tree form a loop in the middle of the line. I prefer to use either an Alpine Butterfly or Prusik loop for this.

2 - Feed the free end of the rope through the remaining tree saver strap, on the opposite end of the first tree, and then bring the rope back and feed the free end through the loop. NOTE: Using a carabiner will reduce friction and wear of the rope.

3 - Using the mid-line loop as a pulley, pull with the free end until the desired tension has been reached and secure the knot with two Half Hitches wrapping around both lines.
See also Highline

U

URBAN TRAILS

Despite spending on average over 30 nights a year in backcountry wilderness camps, I consider myself primarily a front country rider. The local suburban trail systems are some of the first places that my animals visit after completing their initial training. The hikers, bikers, strollers, etc., that we encounter are good practice for desensitizing. Local areas also make excellent locations for getting everyone in good physical shape for longer excursions.

VARIATION

The difference between true north and the direction your compass needle points to is called variation, or declination. The variance may be 20 or more degrees and, if not accounted for, can cause you to be very late for dinner. Learn how to use your compass properly and ensure that you're back in camp before dinner is over.

See also Declination, Navigation

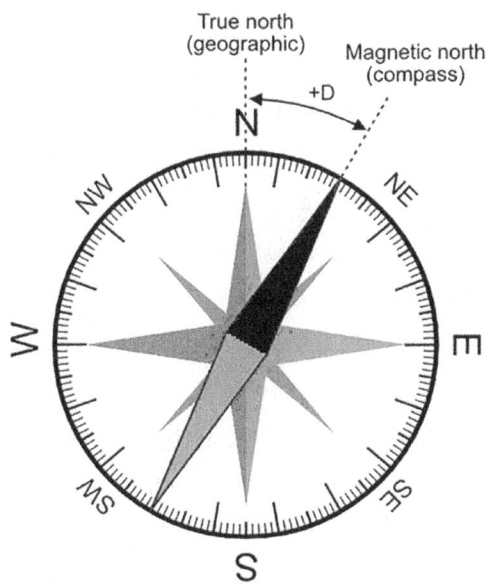

VITAL SIGNS OF THE ADULT HORSE

Do you know your horse's normal vital signs? Vital signs include your horse's resting heart rate, breathing rate, and temperature. A change in your horse's vital signs could be an indication of a health problem. You'll be better prepared to recognize when something may be wrong if you learn your horse's typical vital signs when at rest and after exercise.

> PRO TIP
> # Ask your veterinarian to teach you how to take your horse's vitals.

Normal vital signs for adult horses (at rest):

- Heart rate 38-44 beats per minute.
- Rectal temperature 99.5 - 102.1 degrees Fahrenheit (37-38.5°C).
- Respiratory (breathing) rate 12-20 breaths per minute.
- Gums should be light pink, moist, and have a capillary refill time under 2 seconds.
- Sounds of the intestines should be heard on both sides of the abdomen. Gurgling, gas-like growls, tinkling sounds, and occasional roars are normal. No intestinal sounds or decreased intestinal sounds could be a sign of colic.
- A healthy horse will pass manure eight to 12 times a day. Urine should be wheat-colored and either clear or slightly cloudy.
- The average horse drinks between five and 10 gallons of water a day, depending on exercise level and weather conditions.

If you suspect your horse is colicking or having some other sort of health issue, of course, you'll want to contact your veterinarian. But don't be surprised if some of their first questions involve your horse's vital signs.

It is important to practice taking vital signs before a health emergency occurs. That way, you're comfortable with the techniques, and you have a baseline for what's normal for your horse.

VOLUNTEERING

Horse trails don't just happen. Although equestrians can be credited with developing many of the nation's earliest trails, the fact is today horse riders must work to protect the access that used to be a given. Volunteer with organizations that build and maintain trails, and advocate for equestrian use, or otherwise work to preserve our natural spaces. Volunteering also builds valuable ties to land managers and other trail-user groups, like hikers and mountain bikers. Every user group has a stake in trails. It benefits all of us, in the long run, to get along and share these resources.

WALK

There's no shame in dismounting and walking. Anyone who says otherwise is silly. Whether it's to stretch your legs, give your horse a well-earned break, or because it was scary to be high above the ground on the back of a horse, there are perfectly acceptable reasons to get out of the saddle. Before you dismount, be sure that you've trained your horse to respect your space and not crowd you on the ground.

See also Confidence, Training

WATER

Horses and humans require water to operate. It's non-negotiable. Without adequate hydration, we fail. It's up to us humans to plan for a good water supply, whether you're hauling out for a day ride or an extended camping trip. Here's how I ensure my animals have enough water anytime we're away from home.

How much to haul - The average horse requires between 5 to 10 gallons of water every day. I err on the side of caution and plan on 10 gallons per beast per day any time we leave the farm. Beyond a day ride that planning becomes more critical.

Day rides - There may not be water at the trailhead, and trucks can break down on the way home. Carry a day's worth of water, in your truck or trailer, for each animal just in case your day ride becomes something longer. Riders should also consider carrying a collapsible bucket in their saddlebags in case a stream bank is inaccessible during a ride.

Trailhead camping - Check with the land manager to see if there is a water source in camp. Even if the camp has a reliable water source, bring extra water from home in case the well pump fails. If you're traveling to a dry camp without reliable water, you'll have to haul enough for each animal and each day that you plan on camping, as well as extra for the drive home.

Backcountry pack trips – You can't efficiently haul water on the trail and instead must plan your trip around natural water sources. Consult your maps and check with land managers about reliable springs and water sources before your trip.

Hauling Water

Once you've determined how much water your animals will need, you'll have to figure out how best to carry it. There are myriads of ways to haul water from garbage cans lined with plastic bags to built-in tanks in your trailer, but all have the same limitations; weight and the ability to refill.

Water is heavy, weighing over 8.3 pounds per gallon. Hauling any appreciable amount will impact the carrying capacity of your truck and trailer. A 50-gallon tank holds nearly 420 pounds of water, not including the weight of the tank itself. That weight must be accounted for when calculating your vehicle's payload.

The ability to easily refill your water tanks is imperative if you plan on being gone longer than the capacity of your tanks. Most water tanks built for horse trailers have small garden hose-sized openings that are a hassle to refill if you're away from pressurized water sources. Many, if not most, horse camps in the west do not have this type of water source; instead, they mainly rely on well pumps.

Instead of "horse trailer" water tanks we went with food-grade 35-gallon horizontal tanks that feature large top openings that are easy to use when filling with buckets. These tanks live in the truck bed and give us extra storage room in the trailer.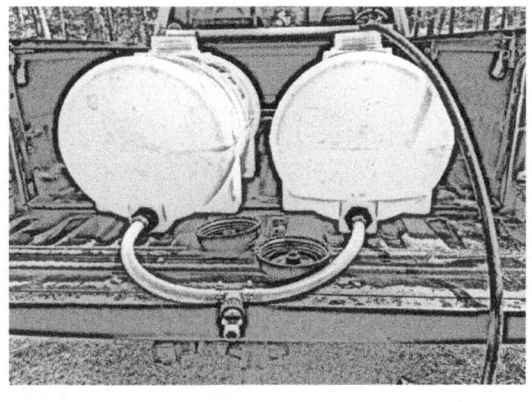

Once you've decided how to transport water, you'll want to consider these additional considerations. Bring your buckets. Try to avoid communal water troughs where diseases may lurk. I don't know if the last horse to visit the trough has had its vaccinations. I don't want to worry about it either. I bring water buckets from home and fill them from the spigot, not the trough.

WATER CROSSING TRAINING

Dihydrogen Monoxide is colorless, odorless, tasteless, and kills uncounted thousands every year. Cocoa knows this and has consistently refused to get anywhere near the stuff. Unfortunately, her job description requires her to frequently cross bodies of the substance.

Dihydrogen (H2) Monoxide (O) is, of course, H2O or water, and water crossings are the bane of many trail riders. Cocoa and I are no exception, as I discovered during one of her first packing experiences. A tiny stream that I could easily step across in one stride and shallow enough that if I were to walk through would not touch the top of my shoes, was enough to derail the ride in short order. Thank you, Cocoa, for the opportunity! Preparing a horse, or mule, to steadily and self-confidently cross water takes planning, patience, and practice. This is how Cocoa and I went from refusing puddles to confidently crossing rivers.

Planning

Nature tells Cocoa that bodies of water are full of alligators, ready and waiting to turn her into lunch. So, she'd much rather stay high and dry, thank you very much. Turning this landlubber into a veritable seahorse required planning, and forethought. Living on the edge of a desert, I must drive over an hour to find trails with reliable water crossings. I wanted to recreate easier to get to water obstacles at home. In this case, I started with a tarp and a running hose. After that hurdle, we progressed to a natural depression in the ground that I filled with water. Neither of these bears much resemblance to a moving stream, but they're the closest I have without driving or hiring an excavator. Once Cocoa is doing well with our faux stream, we'll start hauling to an actual river and continue our training efforts there.

Patience

Cocoa's fear of strange water is natural, and I want to use our training to fill in the Cocoa coloring book with as many positive experiences as possible. To me, this means looking at our training efforts as an ongoing process vs. a singular event and using methods that acclimate her to new challenges in degrees.

In this, I try to make our desired outcome, "crossing the water", the easiest solution. For example, as long as Cocoa is facing the water, we're good. When she plants her feet and refuses to step forward willingly, we move our feet. I may not be able to make her step forward, but I can certainly make her take a step to one side or another. In the process, she'll move ever so slightly closer to her imaginary water hazard. With every step closer to the water, I release the pressure and praise her. I call keeping her feet moving when she's not ready to stand quietly in the water, the yoyo game.

Once she's relaxed, we try for one more step closer and then another. Then another after that.

Practice

Once we've gotten that first crossing under our belt (or is that cinch?), it's time to reinforce the skill with practice and grow the size of Cocoa's happy place. Once she was good with a watery tarp, we moved to a water-filled depression in the yard, then to a small rivulet in a trail, then to an honest-to-goodness river crossing. Each subsequent success is built upon the accomplishment of the obstacle before it. By varying the type of water obstacle (depth, current, clear vs. muddy, narrow stream vs. wide river), I'm teaching Cocoa that water is water regardless of the type, and I believe that this generalization will help us when approaching different water passages in the future.

Water crossings are going to happen. We'll all be better off if we take the time and effort to acquaint our horses and mules to this fact of trail riding now and on our terms.

My method seeks to avoid a battle of the wills and instead tries to make the obstacle an area of rest and relaxation. It takes time but avoids drama.

See also Training

WEATHER

Some days it seems like the weather has gone crazy. It often feels hard to predict what kind of weather we might have this afternoon, let alone tomorrow or next week. Fortunately, there's a lot of info to glean for ourselves just by looking up to the sky. Yes, you can be a meteorologist. Clouds provide accurate indicators of the weather to come. If we know what to look for in the sky, the clouds will tell us what kind of weather to expect. This forecasting helps us to be

ABCs of Horse Camping

prepared for when we're planning a trip, on a trail ride, or while horse camping. We've been attempting to forecast the weather since we crawled out of the sea. Long before the invention of modern meteorological tools, people relied upon natural clues to approaching weather. All these clues have a scientific basis that explains why they work.

The first recorded use of weather folklore is found in the Bible. In Matthew 16.2-3, Jesus says to the fishermen, "when it is evening, you say, 'It will be fair weather, for the sky is red.' and in the morning, 'It will be stormy today, for the sky is red and threatening." Similar sayings include: "Red sky in morning, sailors take warning. Red sky at night, sailors' delight.", and "Evening red and morning gray, help the traveler on his way. Evening gray and morning red brings down a rain upon his head."

Here's the science behind those well-known sayings: A red sky at night (when the sun is to the west) is caused by light passing through dust particles in the air to the west. Dust indicates dry weather and since most weather changes come from the west, a red sky at night usually indicates dry weather approaching. A red sky in the morning, however, indicates that the dry air has moved away. A gray sky at night means that the western air is filled with moisture, and it will likely rain soon.

Here are more weather rhymes and proverbs to remember, as well as what the clouds tell us about the weather to help you be a better weathercaster.

Cumulus - Latin Derivative: "Heap"

Throughout the world, one of the most favored clouds among people in the outdoors is the cumulus cloud. The puffy, fluffy, whimsical clouds add character to beautiful sunny days and are often associated with pleasant weather. When cumulus clouds are in view, the forecast is as threatening as the mashed potatoes they resemble.

Stratus - Latin Derivative: "Layer"

Stratus clouds are flat and featureless and often completely blanket the sky on a gray day. These thick, heavy, gray clouds dominate the sky, and the darker the shade of gray, the higher the moisture content. While they usually don't indicate extreme weather, be prepared for rain with this cloud type.

Rhymes to Remember: "Ring around the moon? Rain real soon." For ages, sailors have known that a halo around the sun or moon is the harbinger of bad weather. A ring around the moon usually indicates an advancing warm front, which means precipitation. Likewise, when you see a halo around the sun, you should expect rainy weather in a day or two. The clouds that create these halos are very high-altitude stratus clouds known as cirrostratus clouds. These clouds lack definition and usually appear from the ground as a thin haze. They are full of moisture, and when they arrive, rain usually isn't far behind.

Cirrus - Latin Derivative: "Curl of hair"

These are the high, wispy clouds that make for beautiful sunsets. Cirrus clouds live very high in the atmosphere and are made up of tiny ice crystals. They form ahead of warm fronts and are indicative of upcoming precipitation. While cirrus clouds may filter sunshine and make for a beautiful day, don't be fooled...they can indicate impending storms!

Rhymes to Remember: "Trace in the sky the painter's brush, the winds around you soon will rush." – "Mares' tails make lofty ships carry low sails."

Nimbus - Latin Derivative: "Violent rain"

Nimbus clouds refer to any of the above clouds which have taken on a dark color, thus indicating high moisture levels within the cloud and rain to come. For example, a cumulonimbus cloud is a cumulus cloud that is uncharacteristically dark and foreboding and is associated with thunderstorms. Cumulonimbus clouds often rise like towers into the sky and sometimes take the shape of an anvil, with the longer end of the anvil head typically pointing in the direction the storm is heading. So, when rocks, towers, or anvils appear in the sky, expect storms.

Rhymes to Remember: "When clouds appear like rocks and towers, the earth is refreshed with frequent showers."

I hope this short guide helps you to be a better amateur meteorologist.

WEED FREE FEED

You've most likely heard the terms "weed-free feed" or "certified weed-free forage". In a growing number of areas, weed-free feed is required. Whether or not this specially certified feed for horses is required or simply requested where you ride, it's a good idea to have a basic level of knowledge about what these feeds are and, more importantly, what feeds fulfill the requirements. No one wants to have an enjoyable camping trip cut short by a hefty fine for not complying with the rules.

The problem of invasive species is very real and has been described as the largest conservation concern of the 21st century. The fiscal impacts of invasive species pack a big punch: Invasive species are now found in all 50 states, and published reports estimate the negative economic impact to be as much as $138 billion annually. To combat the threat, agencies across the US have responded aggressively. This has profoundly affected recreational stock users.

There are currently several types of weed-free feed that meet federal and state requirements. Forage, unprocessed hay and some processed feeds such as cubes and pellets must meet the standards of the North American Weed Management Association (NAWMA).

Certified noxious weed seed-free hay bales are distinguished by a

bale tag or unique color twine and represent a hayfield that has been inspected by the state agriculture department for noxious weeds. Bales of certified hay can be the size and weight of a normal bale or a "double pressed" form that is half the size of a regular bale but contains the same amount of hay by weight.

A significant advantage of unprocessed hay, from a dietary standpoint, is the fiber length of the hay stems. Greater fiber length takes horses longer to chew and digest; this keeps their mouths and digestive systems full and working longer. Longer fiber length also helps keep a horse warmer in cold weather. The major disadvantage of baled or unprocessed hay is the weight and bulk of the hay bales when packing into camp. Many people find the heavier hay bales cumbersome. Also, there tends to be more waste when using unprocessed forage. Certified weed-free hay cubes and pellets are minimally processed feeds that have been chopped and then heat-pressure treated into a cube or pellet. Bags of certified noxious weed-free cubes or pellets will be labeled with a certification stating compliance with the North American Weed Free Forage Certification Program. Compared to baled hay, pellets and cubes create less mess and waste. In addition, the packaging of a processed product makes it easier to transport. Less waste and increased digestibility mean that a fifty-pound bag of pellets could last as long as a sixty- or seventy-pound hay bale.

Commercially processed feed pellets are processed by finely grinding the ingredients, heat treating, and then compressing them into pellets. These complete feeds (usually in large or small pellet form) in which ground hay is balanced with grains for energy, vitamins, and minerals are designed to replace a 100% hay or pasture diet. Nutritionally speaking, the processed feeds have a guaranteed nutrient content. Equine nutritionists formulate and balance the fiber, energy, protein, vitamins, and mineral sources in these feeds to provide a complete feed and eliminate the need for additional grain or supplements.

Of course, cubes and pellets have disadvantages as well. First, horses and mules drink considerably more water when eating pellets and cubes due to the decreased water content of the product. So be sure to provide fresh, clean water at all times to reduce the chance of colic. Also, there is a slightly increased chance of choking on pellets and cubes, especially if you have an enthusiastic eater. You can decrease the chances of this and provide extra water to your horse by soaking the pellets or cubes for 10-30 minutes before feeding. The second disadvantage to pellets or cubes is the decreased intake time. Most horses will quickly consume these, leaving your horse standing around without much to do. The processing of the product also makes it digest faster, which leaves your horse's stomach empty for a longer period.

As to which weed-free option to use during your next trip into a regulated area. Unprocessed feeds are more similar to your horse's usual feed but may be more difficult to find. Commercially processed feeds are readily available but don't provide the roughage that an equine gut is designed to digest. Many experienced horse campers will take and use all three. I generally take hay for use at the trailhead and sometimes pack in cubes or pellets in the backcountry.

Regardless of which type of feeds you decide on, make sure that any tags or certification certificates stay with the feedbags in case a ranger or land manager asks to verify certification. Also, if you're changing your horse's diet, it's best to begin gradually. Start changing over to the new feed days in advance so your horse can get used to the new diet. Sudden feed changes have been known to cause colic and an expensive veterinary visit.

Decide which method of feeding your horse certified weed-free product is best for your situation by weighing the convenience of a packaged product to the fiber length of the hay bale. Whichever choice you make, have fun enjoying camping with your horse.
See also Feed

WILDERNESS

In 1964, the Wilderness Act was passed and signed into law by President Lyndon B. Johnson. This act was the result of a long effort to protect and promote wilderness areas across the U.S. In a time of legislative and administrative excesses, the act is refreshing in its succinct and almost poetic definition of wilderness. "A wilderness, in contrast with those areas where man and his own works dominate the landscape, is hereby recognized as an area where the earth and its community of life are untrammeled by man, where man himself is a visitor who does not remain." It is a wonderful place to visit on the back of a willing horse or mule.

GRASS CAMP TRAIL
NO. 1219

X

XENOPHON

Xenophon Son of Gryllus, Athenian, and author of "On the Art of Horsemanship". This treatise was published in 360 BCE and is the oldest known text on horsemanship. The principles that he described have been used by equestrian enthusiasts for the past 2,300 years. From modern-day trainers to the foundations of dressage, his insights have formed the equestrian world as we know it. A copy of this seminal work belongs on the bookshelf of every horse owner.

Y

YOUNG

A young mule, like an inexperienced rider, is a very teachable creature. The two creatures shouldn't be too close together as they will most certainly teach one another bad habits. In short, young animals and green horsemen equals a black and blue rider.

If you're a novice rider, a mature horse with training and trail experience behind him will have most of the buggers already worked out of his system and will help teach you many of the joys of trail riding.

Z

Zip. That's it. Thanks for reading, now go out and ride!

Checklist – Trail Ride

Trail Rider Checklist – From www.TrailMeister.com
Your Where to Ride Guide

In the Truck / Trailer
- [ ] Road Map and Directions to trailhead
- [ ] Registration / Insurance
- [ ] Coggins Papers / Health Papers/Brand Inspection
- [ ] Flashlight w/ spare batteries
- [ ] Spare Tire Truck / Trailer
- [ ] Jack & Lug Wrench - Truck and Trailer
- [ ] Chock Blocks for Wheels
- [ ] Manure Rake / Forks
- [ ] Manure bucket
- [ ] Spares
  - Extra Cinch / Girth
  - Headstall / Bridle
  - Reins
  - Halter and Lead
- [ ] Tools – Pliers / Screwdriver
- [ ] Duct tape
- [ ] Garbage bags

_____

Tack
- [ ] Saddle
- [ ] Bridle
- [ ] Saddle Pads
- [ ] Saddle / Pommel Bags
- [ ] Halter
- [ ] Hobbles
- [ ] Breast Collar
- [ ] Crupper / Breechin
- [ ] Cinch / Girth
- [ ] ID tag

_____

Equine Supplies
- [ ] Feed – Hay / Grain
- [ ] Feed and Water Buckets
- [ ] Water
- [ ] Hay Bag
- [ ] Horse First Aid Kit
- [ ] Fly Spray
- [ ] Hoof Pick
- [ ] Sponge or rag
- [ ] Grooming Supplies
- [ ] Hoof Rasp

_____
_____

Personal Supplies
- [ ] Riding Pants and Jeans
- [ ] Riding Boots
- [ ] Socks
- [ ] Outerwear Jacket / Sweater
- [ ] Rain Gear
- [ ] Undergarments
- [ ] Extra Set of Keys
- [ ] Knife
- [ ] Lip Balm
- [ ] Hat - Gloves
- [ ] Helmet
- [ ] Sun Block
- [ ] Insect Repellent
- [ ] First Aid Kit
- [ ] Toilet Paper / Wet Ones
- [ ] Medications
- [ ] ID for emergencies

_____
_____
_____

On the Trail
- [ ] Hoof Pick
- [ ] Knife / Wire Cutters
- [ ] Map of the area / Compass
- [ ] Water Bottle
- [ ] Snacks
- [ ] Saddle Bag / Pommel Bags
- [ ] Helmet
- [ ] Insect Repellent
- [ ] First Aid Kit
- [ ] Rain Slicker
- [ ] Cell Phone/way to call for help
- [ ] Rope/ cord for repairs
- [ ] Lead rope
- [ ] Sun Block
- [ ] Camera
- [ ] Lighter
- [ ] Flashlight

_____

Camp Equipment
- [ ] Tent / Hammock
- [ ] Sleeping bag
- [ ] Camp Shoes/Mud Boots
- [ ] Lantern
- [ ] Food
- [ ] Camp Stove
- [ ] Air mattress
- [ ] Saw
- [ ] First Aid Kit
- [ ] Insect Repellent
- [ ] Camp Chairs
- [ ] Folding table
- [ ] Highline gear

_____
_____

Trail Rider Checklist – From www.TrailMeister.com - World's Largest Horse Trail and Camp Guide
Rev2 20181108

Checklist – Trailer Toolkit

Trailer Toolkit Checklist – From www.TrailMeister.com
Your Where to Ride Guide

Vacation Savers to Keep in Your Truck / Trailer

4 Essentials	10 Tools	9 Tire Changing Tools
☐ Fire extinguisher	☐ Screwdrivers (Phillips & Flat)	☐ Roadside triangles
☐ Jumper cables	☐ Pliers	☐ Reflective safety vest
☐ Jump start battery pack	☐ Channel-lock pliers	☐ Wheel chocks
☐ First aid kit	☐ Adjustable crescent wrench	☐ Trailer aid
	☐ Claw hammer	☐ Lug wrench
3 Connecting Items	☐ Pocket knife	☐ Can of Fix a Flat
☐ Glue	☐ Wire cutters	☐ Gloves
☐ Zip ties	☐ Tape measure	☐ Tire pressure gauge
☐ Duct tape	☐ Mini hacksaw	☐ Portable air compressor
	☐ Folding Saw	
		MISC. Add Your Own
5 to Keep the Lights on	**3 Optional**	☐
☐ Electrical tape	☐ Multi tool	☐
☐ Spare fuses	☐ Permanent marker	☐
☐ Spare bulbs	☐ Communications device	☐
☐ LED flashlight		☐
☐ Multi-meter		☐
		☐
		☐

Form - Emergency Plan

Ride Emergency Plan
From www.TrailMeister.com – Your where to ride guide

If you have not heard from me by (time) _____ of (day) _____ of (month)_____, please contact search and rescue at 911 and report me as overdue. Provide search and rescue with ALL of the information below.

Time/date of Departure: _____   Expected Time/date of Return: _____

Names (include your own)	Age	Phone#	Physical Description	Medical issues / medications

Emergency Equipment Carried: ☐ - 1st Aid Kit ☐ - Flashlight ☐ - Map ☐ - Compass ☐ - Knife ☐ - Water ☐ - Food ☐ - Communications ☐ - Lighter/matches ☐ - Rain gear ☐ - Medications
Other: _____

Vehicle / Trailer	Make	Color	License #

Equine	Sex	Description	Age	Breed	Shod	Brands

Veterinarian:_____ Vet Contact info: _____
Farrier: _____ Farrier Contact info: _____

In Case of Emergency (ICE) – Name- Relationship – Contact information: _____
_____

Trip Details: Activity Type: ☐ day ride   ☐ camping

Trailhead Name: _____ State: ___ Address / Coordinates: _____

Planned Trails and Route: _____
_____
_____

Backup Plan: _____
_____
_____

Additional Trip Notes: _____
_____

Ride Emergency Planning Document – From www.TrailMeister.com – World's Largest Horse Trail and Camp Guide

ABCs of Horse Camping

Online Resources

Guide to Horse Trails and Camps
www.TrailMeister.com

Video Aids

How to Tie the Bowline
www.trailmeister.com/how-to-tie-a-bowline/

A Better Highline
www.trailmeister.com/a-better-highline/

Hobble Training
www.trailmeister.com/hobble-training-for-horses/

Pony with Confidence
www.trailmeister.com/how-to-pony-with-confidence/

Trailer Maintenance
www.trailmeister.com/trailer-maintenance/

About the Author

Writing a book is more complicated than I imagined and more satisfying than I could have believed.

Robert Eversole is an internationally recognized clinician who emphasizes practical horsemanship and outdoor skills in his clinics on trail riding and camping with horses. A refugee from corporate America, Robert built the world's largest guide to horse trails and camps, www.TrailMeister.com, when he found that accurate information was unavailable. In his clinics and trail riding columns in leading equine publications, Robert draws from his experiences as a veteran of the US Marine Corps, a PATH-certified instructor, and decades teaching equestrian and outdoor skills. He lives in the Pacific Northwest with his wife, three mules, a horse, and a dog named Boo.

Made in United States
Orlando, FL
08 May 2022

17666910R00189